Legal English

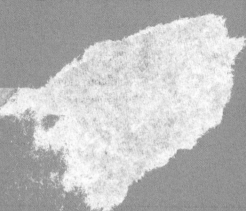

Legal English

How to Understand and Master the Language of Law

William R. McKay and
Helen E. Charlton

PEARSON
Longman

Harlow, England • London • New York • Boston • San Francisco • Toronto
Sydney • Tokyo • Singapore • Hong Kong • Seoul • Taipei • New Delhi
Cape Town • Madrid • Mexico City • Amsterdam • Munich • Paris • Milan

Pearson Education Limited

Edinburgh Gate
Harlow
Essex CM20 2JE
England

and Associated Companies throughout the world

Visit us on the World Wide Web at:
www.pearsoned.co.uk

_____

Published 2005

ISBN 0-582-89436-0

British Library Cataloguing-in-Publication Data
A catalogue record for this book is available from the British Library

Library of Congress Cataloging-in-Publication Data
A catalog record for this book is available from the Library of Congress

10 9 8 7 6 5 4 3 2 1
08 07 06 05

Typeset in 10/13pt Palatino by 69
Printed by Ashford Colour Press Ltd, Gosport

The publisher's policy is to use paper manufactured from sustainable forests.

Table of contents

Acknowledgements

The publishers and authors would like to thank the following individuals and publications for granting permission to reproduce copyright material.

Employment Tribunals Service for permission to include sample copies of Employment Tribunal forms.

The *Law Society Gazette* for permission to reproduce the following articles:

- 'Shopping Around' (edition dated 4 March 2004)
- 'Having cross words in the courtroom' (edition dated 1 April 2004)
- 'Asian tigers prepare to spring' (edition dated 20 May 2004).

Nigel Hanson for permission to reproduce 'Shopping Around'. Nigel Hanson is a member of the media team at Foot Anstey Sargent.

Justin Michaelson (Weil, Gotshal & Manges) on behalf of the Solicitors' Association of Higher Court Advocates, for permission to reproduce 'Having cross words in the courtroom'.

Lucy Trevelyan for permission to reproduce 'Asian tigers prepare to spring'.

Margot Taylor, Principal Lecturer at the Inns of Court School of Law, for permission to reproduce her article entitled 'Which route – solicitor or barrister?' (*The Times*, 20 January 2004).

The authors would also like to express their gratitude to Sharon Hanson and David Ronson for providing valued comments and feedback in the course of this book being written.

Publisher's note

Introduction

This book has been written to assist those interested in law and wishing to become more conversant in English within a legal context (whether as a native English speaker or someone using English as a second or foreign language). It is therefore intended to be of assistance to a variety of individuals, including:

- those aiming to study or presently studying law within an English language jurisdiction (whether for academic or vocational training purposes)
- those presently involved in the legal or business domain whose work brings them into contact with legal practice.

Communication skills in oral and written legal English are developed through a programme of language activity in conjunction with key legal skills training including:

- advocacy
- interviewing and advising
- negotiation
- legal writing and drafting

In this way this publication offers the reader stimulating and enjoyable instruction designed to progressively enhance relevant and meaningful communication skills in oral and written legal English. Such a task based approach enables the reader to optimise academic and professional effectiveness, offering a valuable source for academic and professional development. *Legal English* provides the opportunity to build on language skills in a professional context through familiarisation with realistic legal scenarios and materials prepared by a qualified lawyer. The exercises are suited to both self-study and group study in a classroom.

Readers therefore benefit from pro-active skills based exercises. These involve the use of realistic legal precedents to develop a working knowledge of legal practice and ability in performing 'real-life' legal tasks and procedures – all in the context of improving the reader's ability to use legal English.

English is predominantly the language of international legal practice and its importance to lawyers cannot be over-emphasised. The way in which one uses legal English can therefore be crucial to professional success. Competence is developed throughout the book in a logical sequence of ascending complexity. Exercises are also cumulative, previous lessons being reinforced and built upon in subsequent exercises while also containing a practice and feedback element.

1

The book consists of main sections on:

- Litigation (including courtroom advocacy, court orders, court documentation, paperwork used by court lawyers, case preparation and problem solving)
- Business law (including company documentation, company meetings and resolutions and commercial agreements)

These sections also include an explanation of basic legal principles (such as in relation to the law of contract and tort) as well as a review of language and grammar – all in the context of 'portable' skills training which will be of value in many academic and professional contexts.

Additional sections on journalistic texts and legal research and study guidance further contribute to making this a book of much value to readers wishing to develop their legal English for use in the course of legal study or practice. It offers a stimulating and enjoyable learning resource and can be used by readers with or without any legal training. It will be of most use however to readers with at least an upper intermediate standard in English language.

In each chapter you will be provided with an introduction to a different legal topic. You are then provided with a range of language exercises relating to the legal topic for that chapter.

These exercises involve legal skills practise and role-play (such as advocacy, interviewing, negotiation and writing/drafting), enabling you to develop your proficiency in legal English. The areas of language and law in each chapter are then summarised to consolidate your learning. Answers to the exercises are provided in Appendix 3 and should be checked only after you have undertaken the exercises.

For further resources see www.pearsoned.co.uk/McKay

PART 1
Business law and practice

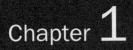

Chapter 1 Company formation

Learning Objectives

By completing the exercises in this chapter you will:

■ Acquire knowledge of the legal characteristics and nature of a limited company
■ Acquire an appreciation of the vocabulary and grammar relevant to company law
■ Become aware of the information required in order to incorporate a company
■ Understand and be capable of explaining the legal procedures and documentation required for company formation
■ Be able to prepare the legal documentation necessary in order to create a company

Company law

Characteristics of a company

A company is regarded in law as being a separate legal 'person', with a separate legal personality. This means that it has rights separate from its owners and managers to enter into contracts, employ people, own property and conduct business. The creation and management of a company is governed by the Companies Act 1985 (CA '85) and the Companies Act 1989.

By far the largest number of incorporated companies are incorporated with limited liability, being limited by shares as defined by section 1(2)(a) CA '85. The potential financial liability of a member (in other words shareholder) in such a company is limited to the amount, if any, remaining unpaid on the shares held by that particular member. Such a company is known as a limited company and will have the word 'Limited' at the end of its name.

A company can be a private or a public company. A public company must have a minimum issued share capital of £50,000, as required by sections 11 and 118 CA '85. A public company may offer its shares for sale to the public (s. 81 CA '85), whereas a private company must not. A public company may also have its shares listed (and traded) on the Stock Exchange. Information on the current values of such listed shares is publicly available and can be checked for instance in *The Financial Times*.

Exercise 1 – reading

COMPANY FORMATION

There are a number of legal requirements which must be complied with in order to incorporate (in other words create) a company. In particular, the following documentation will normally be required.

Memorandum of Association

The Memorandum of Association (known as the 'articles of incorporation' in the US) contains the following information:

■ Name of the company
■ The company's objects and powers (meaning basically the sphere of activities and nature of the company)
■ The company's share capital

Articles of Association

The Articles of Association (the articles) are in effect a set of rules governing the conduct of the members of the company and its officers. The officers of a company are its directors and company secretary. These rules commonly relate to matters such as the conduct of share-holder and board meetings, any restriction on the transferability of shares and the powers bestowed on the directors etc. (In the US the Articles of Association are known as the bylaws.) Many companies use a standard form of articles known as 'Table A Articles'.

Form 10

This is a standard form which must be completed with details of the intended officers of the company, as required by s. 10(2) CA '85. Every incorporated company must have at least one director and one company secretary. (If there is to be only one director then that individual cannot also be the company secretary.) Details of the company's registered office (at which formal documents will usually be served upon the company) should also be included in Form 10.

Form 12

This is another standard form which must be signed by a person applying for incorporation of the company to certify that the legal requirements for registration have been complied with. The person signing Form 12 (commonly known as the promoter of the company) can be one of the directors, the company secretary or a solicitor engaged in the formation of the company.

Once completed, these company documents must then be sent to the Registrar of Companies ('the registrar'), along with a fee. The registrar then registers the company and issues a Certificate of Incorporation. This is when the company comes into existence. There are further legal requirements which the incorporated company must then continue to comply with, such as having annual accounts prepared (s. 226 CA '85), a copy of which must be filed annually at Companies House (s. 242 CA '85).

▌ Language practice

Exercise 2 – comprehension

Answer the following questions concerning company formation, based on the above information.

1. What is meant by 'limited liability'?
2. What is the minimum amount of issued share capital which a public company must maintain?
3. List the four documents normally required in order to form a company.
4. If a client wishes to incorporate a company and be its only director, can s/he also be the company secretary? If not then explain why not.
5. Name the document issued by the Registrar of Companies which is in effect a 'birth certificate' for a new company.

Exercise 3 – drafting

Now assume that you are a lawyer in the Business Law Department of Stringwoods & Evans, a city law firm located at 18 Bond Street, London, W1 1KR (telephone number 020 7538 2892; DX number 12432, London 1). You have been instructed by a new client named Thomas Shapiro (TS) to incorporate a company for him. TS is a successful entrepreneur with business interests throughout Europe and the Far East. He now wishes to establish a private company limited by shares to be named 'Maplink Limited'. Maplink Limited will be run as a business, publishing various maps and guides for tourists visiting London and other cities around the world.

Your senior partner has already drafted the Articles of Association for Maplink Limited. You are now required to complete the further documentation needed to form the company. This consists of:

■ The Memorandum of Association
■ Form 10
■ Form 12

Taking account of the company details provided on p. 8, complete the following company formation documentation accordingly by entering the correct details in the shaded spaces.

▶

MAPLINK LIMITED – COMPANY PROFILE

REGISTERED OFFICE	44 Princess Diana Walk, South Kensington, London, W2 3SL (Telephone no. 020 7429 8137)
DIRECTORS	(1) MR THOMAS SHAPIRO of 23 Essex Street, Hampton Court, Surrey, KT8 1NQ (Barrister – date of birth 12 February 1968)
	(2) PROFESSOR DIMITRIS YAVAPRAPAS of 'The Manor', 2 Queen Elizabeth Street, London, SE1 5NP (Surgeon - date of birth 3 July 1954)
COMPANY SECRETARY	MISS GISELA WIRTH of 15 Robin Hood Way, Mansfield, Nottingham, NG2 7CX (Accountant, date of birth 28 November 1973)
AUTHORISED SHARE CAPITAL	250,000 X £1 Ordinary Shares
MEMBERS AND SHAREHOLDINGS	THOMAS SHAPIRO 175,000
	DIMITRIS YAVAPRAPAS 50,000
	GISELA WIRTH 25,000

THE COMPANIES ACTS 1985 TO 1989

PRIVATE COMPANY LIMITED BY SHARES

MEMORANDUM OF ASSOCIATION OF _____ [1]

1. The Company's name is _____. [2]
2. The Company's registered office is to be situated in England and Wales.
3. The object of the Company is to carry on business as a general commercial company.
4. The liability of the Members is _____. [3]
5. The Company's share capital is £ _____ [4] divided into 250,000 ordinary shares of £1 each.

WE the subscribers to this Memorandum of Association wish to form into a Company pursuant to this Memorandum and we agree to take the number of shares shown opposite our respective names.

Names and addresses of Subscribers	Number of shares taken by each subscriber
THOMAS SHAPIRO	
23 ESSEX STREET,	
HAMPTON COURT,	
SURREY, KT8 1NQ	ONE HUNDRED AND SEVENTY-FIVE THOUSAND

1 _____ [5]
_____
_____
_____

FIFTY THOUSAND

2 _____ [6]
_____
_____
_____   3 _____ [7]

Total shares taken :   4 _____ [8]

Dated this 15 th. day of May 20 06

10

Companies House
— for the record —

Please complete in typescript,
or in bold black capitals.
CHWP000

Notes on completion appear on final page

First directors and secretary and intended situation of registered office

Company Name in full

Proposed Registered Office

(PO Box numbers only, are not acceptable)

Post town

County / Region   Postcode

If the memorandum is delivered by an agent for the subscriber(s) of the memorandum mark the box opposite and give the agent's name and address.

Agent's Name

Address

Post town

County / Region   Postcode

Number of continuation sheets attached

You do not have to give any contact information in the box opposite but if you do, it will help Companies House to contact you if there is a query on the form. The contact information that you give will be visible to searchers of the public record.

Tel

DX number   DX exchange

Companies House receipt date barcode

This form has been provided free of charge by Companies House

v 08/02

When you have completed and signed the form please send it to the Registrar of Companies at:
Companies House, Crown Way, Cardiff, CF14 3UZ   DX 33050 Cardiff
for companies registered in England and Wales
or
Companies House, 37 Castle Terrace, Edinburgh, EH1 2EB
for companies registered in Scotland   DX 235 Edinburgh
or LP - 4 Edinburgh 2

Company Secretary (see notes 1-5)

Company name

NAME *Style / Title *Honours etc

* Voluntary details Forename(s)

Surname

Previous forename(s)

Previous surname(s)

†† Tick this box if the address shown is a service address for the beneficiary of a Confidentiality Order granted under section 723B of the Companies Act 1985 otherwise, give your usual residential address. In the case of a corporation or Scottish firm, give the registered or principal office address.

Address ††

Post town

County / Region Postcode

Country

I consent to act as secretary of the company named on page 1

Consent signature **Date**

Directors (see notes 1-5)

Please list directors in alphabetical order

NAME *Style / Title *Honours etc

Forename(s)

Surname

Previous forename(s)

Previous surname(s)

†† Tick this box if the address shown is a service address for the beneficiary of a Confidentiality Order granted under section 723B of the Companies Act 1985 otherwise, give your usual residential address. In the case of a corporation or Scottish firm, give the registered or principal office address.

Address ††

Post town

County / Region Postcode

Country

Day Month Year

Date of birth **Nationality**

Business occupation

Other directorships

I consent to act as director of the company named on page 1

Consent signature **Date**

Directors (see notes 1-5)

Please list directors in alphabetical order

| | NAME | *Style / Title | | *Honours etc | |

* Voluntary details

	Forename(s)	
	Surname	YAVAPRAPAS
	Previous forename(s)	
	Previous surname(s)	

†† Tick this box if the address shown is a service address for the beneficiary of a Confidentiality Order granted under section 723B of the Companies Act 1985 otherwise, give your usual residential address. In the case of a corporation or Scottish firm, give the registered or principal office address.

	Address ††	
	Post town	
	County / Region		Postcode	
	Country	

| | Day Month Year | |
| | Date of birth | | Nationality | |

| | Business occupation | |

| | Other directorships | |
| | | |

I consent to act as director of the company named on page 1

| | Consent signature | | Date | |

This section must be signed by either an agent on behalf of all subscribers or the subscribers (i.e those who signed as members on the memorandum of association).

Signed		Date	
Signed		Date	
Signed		Date	
Signed		Date	
Signed		Date	
Signed		Date	
Signed		Date	

Companies House
— for the record —

Please complete in typescript,
or in bold black capitals.

CHWP000

12

Declaration on application for registration

Company Name in full

[1]

I, Thomas Shapiro

of 23 Essex Street, Hampton Court, Surrey

† Please delete as appropriate.

do solemnly and sincerely declare that I am a † [Solicitor engaged in the formation of the company][person named as director or secretary of the company in the statement delivered to the Registrar under section 10 of the Companies Act 1985] and that all the requirements of the Companies Act 1985 in respect of the registration of the above company and of matters precedent and incidental to it have been complied with.

And I make this solemn Declaration conscientiously believing the same to be true and by virtue of the Statutory Declarations Act 1835.

Declarant's signature Thomas Shapiro

Declared at 44 Princess Diana Walk, S. Kensington, London

On | 1 | 5 | 0 | 5 | 2 | 0 | 0 | 6 |

Day Month Year

❶ Please print name.

before me ❶ Jemima Boerge

Signed Jemima Borge **Date** 15th May 2006

† A Commissioner for Oaths or Notary Public or Justice of the Peace or Solicitor

You do not have to give any contact information in the box opposite but if you do, it will help Companies House to contact you if there is a query on the form. The contact information that you give will be visible to searchers of the public record.

[2]

Tel

DX number   DX exchange

Companies House receipt date barcode

This form has been provided free of charge by Companies House.

Form revised 10/03

When you have completed and signed the form please send it to the Registrar of Companies at:
Companies House, Crown Way, Cardiff, CF14 3UZ   DX 33050 Cardiff
for companies registered in England and Wales
or
Companies House, 37 Castle Terrace, Edinburgh, EH1 2EB
for companies registered in Scotland   DX 235 Edinburgh
or LP - 4 Edinburgh 2

Exercise 4 – multi-word verbs

Complete the following sentences by entering an appropriate multi-word verb into each blank space from the selection in the panel below.

contract for	negotiate with	act for
appeal against	decide against	enter into

1. The Defendant has decided to _____ _____ the judgment.
2. The judgment _____ _____ my client.
3. We are confident that the Judge will _____ _____ our opponent.
4. He wants to _____ _____ discussions with a view to becoming a director of the company.
5. He intends to _____ _____ the company to purchase some shares.
6. I have been asked to _____ _____ a newly incorporated company.

Law notes

Characteristics of a limited liability company

- A limited company has a separate legal personality in law (as established by case of *Salomon* v *Salomon* 1897)
- A company is owned by shareholders, management decisions primarily being made by directors
- Shareholders (members) and directors have limited liability
- A company must be registered at the Companies Registry (based in Cardiff for companies incorporated in England and Wales and in Edinburgh for companies incorporated in Scotland)
- A company comes into existence upon issue of a certificate of incorporation
- Documents required to form a company: Memorandum of Association; Articles of Association; Form 10; Form 12
- Memorandum of Association indicates: the name of the company; whether it is a private or public limited company; the objects of the company (which state the purpose of the company and the scope of its legal capacity to conduct business with outside parties)
- Articles of Association provide a set of internal company rules
- A shareholder's personal liability is limited to paying fully for shares held
- A company's nominal (or authorised) share capital refers to the quantity of shares a company is authorised to issue (as indicated in the company's Memorandum of Association)

- A company's issued share capital (also known as allotted share capital) refers to the value of shares actually issued (or allotted) to shareholders
- A company's paid-up share capital refers to the amount of the total (nominal) value of the issued share capital actually 'paid-up' by shareholders
- There are various types of shares which a company can issue, including:
    1. ordinary shares—usually carrying voting rights and a right to any dividend declared by the company (i.e. share of any profits made by the company)
    2. preference shares—which do not carry voting rights (referred to as non-voting shares) but provide priority (i.e. a preference) to payment of a dividend
- Continuing duty on company to maintain annual accounts and to file annual accounts with Registrar of Companies

Grammar notes

Multi-word verbs

Multi-word verbs consist of a verb and at least one particle. A particle is a word which would be a preposition or an adverb in a different context. In this chapter you have encountered several examples of multi-word verbs such as those in:

enter into a contract; comply with the requirements; subscribe their names to.

Multi-word verbs come in four categories:

1. verbs with particles and no object. E.g. *Sit down!*

2. verbs with two particles. E.g. *He gets on with his client.*

3. verb + inseperable particle + object. E.g. *I'm waiting for the trial.*

4. verb + separable particle + object. E.g. *He set out the terms / He set the terms out.*

List of multi-word verbs

The following is a non-exhaustive list of examples of multi-word verbs used in legal English.

act for	appeal against	charge with
contract for	decide for / against	enter into
file for	find against	legislate for / against
negotiate with / for	prohibit from	rule against
settle for	swear in	withdraw from

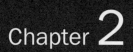

Learning Objectives

By completing the exercises in this chapter you will:

- Understand and be capable of explaining the practice and procedure of board meetings
- Be familiar with board meeting documentation
- Develop your vocabulary in relation to company meetings
- Acquire practice in drafting board meeting documentation
- Develop word skills and vocabulary relevant to company law
- Consider the use of relevant grammar including combining nouns and plural nouns

Introduction

In this chapter and the next one we will consider the practice and procedure of company meetings. These take two basic forms:

1. Board meetings
2. Shareholders' meetings

We shall consider shareholders' meetings in the next chapter. The main characteristics of a board meeting (also known as a directors' meeting) are as follows.

Board meetings

Board meetings are attended by the directors of the company. Day to day business decisions are usually taken at board meetings. Matters to be decided upon are put to the meeting in the form of 'resolutions', each director present casting a vote for or against each resolution being considered. (Voting is usually by a 'show of hands'.) Whether or not a resolution is passed depends on whether the majority of votes are in favour of or against that resolution. In other words the decision is made by a simple majority. Multi-national companies with directors located internationally often stipulate in their articles that board meetings may be validly held by means of telephone or audio-visual conferencing as well as via the internet.

Any director can call a board meeting on reasonable notice to all the other directors. Board meetings are therefore often convened at short notice. A written record is made of matters discussed and of resolutions considered at a board meeting. This record is known as the 'minutes' of the meeting.

Exercise 1 – comprehension

In Chapter 1 we incorporated a company named Maplink Limited ('Maplink'). In common with all companies, Maplink will hold board and shareholders' meetings. Let us assume therefore that Maplink is now planning to hold its first board meeting. (You may recall that Maplink has two directors, namely Thomas Shapiro and Dimitris Yavaprapas.) Continuing to act as Maplink's lawyer you are now asked to prepare the minutes for the first board meeting of the company, taking account of the following specific instructions.

CLIENT INSTRUCTIONS

■ Another director is to be appointed, namely Mr Kadir Salleh of 4 Kensington Palace Gardens, London, W2 4AJ
■ The name of the company is to be changed from Maplink Limited to Travelgraph Limited

TASK

Complete the minutes of the company's first board meeting by selecting the most appropriate word from the list below to place in each correspondingly numbered space in the draft minutes on the following page.

1. (a) restitution (b) resolution (c) resolved (d) determined	5. (a) collated (b) convened (c) assembled (d) accumulated
2. (a) employed (b) appointed (c) selected (d) commissioned	6. (a) given (b) provided (c) catered (d) supplied
3. (a) classified (b) head (c) official (d) registered	7. (a) intentions (b) proposals (c) resolve (d) resolutions
4. (a) disclosed (b) indicated (c) presented (d) represented	8. (a) declared (b) proclaimed (c) affirmed (d) publicised

Now name yourself as the company's solicitor by entering your own name in box 'A' of paragraph 2 of the minutes of the board meeting!

MAPLINK LIMITED

Minutes of the first meeting of the board of directors of Maplink Limited ('the company') held at 44 Princess Diana Walk, South Kensington, London, W2 3SL on 15 May 2006 at 10.00 a.m.

Present: Thomas Shapiro

       Dimitris Yavaprapas

In Attendance: Gisela Wirth

1. Thomas Shapiro and Dimitris Yavaprapas accepted office as directors of the company. It was resolved that Thomas Shapiro be appointed Chairman of the board.

2. It was [1] _____ that [A]_____ be appointed solicitor to the company.

3. It was resolved that Gisela Wirth be [2] _____ secretary of the company.

4. It was resolved that the [3]_____ office be at 44 Princess Diana Walk, South Kensington, London, W2 3SL.

5. It was resolved that the quorum necessary for the transaction of the business of the directors should be two directors personally present.

6. A draft notice of an extraordinary general meeting of the company was [4]_____ to the meeting and approved. It was further resolved that such meeting be [5]_____ and that notice of this be [6]_____ forthwith to the shareholders.

7. The meeting thereupon adjourned. Upon resumption it was reported that the [7]_____ set out in the notice of the extraordinary general meeting had been passed respectively as ordinary and special resolutions of the company.

8. Upon there being no further competent business the meeting was then [8]_____ closed by the Chairman.

_____

Chairman

Exercise 2 – convening a board meeting

Answer the following questions relating to the above text on board meetings and on the minutes you have just finalised for Maplink's first board meeting.

1. What is meant by *convening a meeting*?
2. What is meant by a *simple majority*?
3. What is meant by a vote being taken *on a show of hands*?
4. Why do you think multi-national companies sometimes conduct board meetings by audio-visual conferencing?
5. Suggest one reason why a director may wish to call a board meeting.
6. Paragraph 5 of the minutes indicates that the *quorum* for board meetings is two. What is a quorum?

Law notes

Board meetings

- Attended by directors of the company
- Address general managerial decisions of the company
- Each director normally has one vote
- Only directors of the company can vote at board meetings
- Resolutions are passed by simple majority

Grammar notes

Combining nouns

There are a number of instances in this chapter where two nouns are used together. In such instances the first of the two nouns usually provides some indication or description of the type or variety of the second noun. For example:

a *directors' meeting*   a *shareholders' meeting*

(both a directors' meeting and a shareholders' meeting being *types* of meeting).
Further examples are: *interview record* (a type of record)   *Magistrates' Court* (a type of court)
Sometimes when two nouns are placed together in this way they are separated by a hyphen (-). This often occurs when the two nouns are commonly placed together, as illustrated for instance with *work-place* and *time-limit*. If you are in any doubt as to whether a hyphen is normally used with any particular combination of nouns you are advised to use a good dictionary in order to check, such as *Dictionary of Law* by ▶

L.B. Curzon. Some combinations of nouns have become so synonymous with each other however that they are written as one-word compound nouns. E.g. *wheelchair*.

Possessive forms

Possessive 's'

A possessive 's' is added to nouns along with an apostrophe to indicate that the word(s) following are related (i.e. 'belong') to the word(s) with a possessive 's'. E.g. *counsel's opinion*. The letter 's' is also put at the end of nouns to indicate a range of other relationships. For example:

Places: *Europe's main legal centres*

Time: *four days' trial*

Plural nouns

When dealing with regular plural verbs the apostrophe (') should be placed after the 's'. You will see for instance that this is where the apostrophe is placed with:

directors' meetings　　*shareholders' meetings*

Note that the apostrophe is also placed after the possessive 's' when a singular noun ends in 's'. For instance: *James's case*.

With singular nouns however the apostrophe should be placed before the possessive 's'. Hence:

the expert's report　　*Gordon's witness statement*

This is also the correct position for the apostrophe with irregular plural nouns. E.g. *women's court attire*.

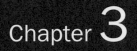

Chapter 3   Shareholders' meetings

Introduction

You will recall that in the last chapter we identified two main types of company meetings:

1. Board meetings (also known as directors' meetings)
2. Shareholders' meetings (also known as members' meetings)

In this chapter we will look at the practice and procedure of the second of these, having considered board meetings in the previous chapter. Read the next section on shareholders' meetings then try the exercises which follow.

Exercise 1 – reading

SHAREHOLDERS' MEETINGS

Company law dictates that certain business decisions concerning a company need shareholder approval. In particular, shareholders' meetings are required when major changes to the company are being proposed. Proposals for such changes are put to a shareholders' meeting in the form of resolutions. Shareholders' meetings can be attended by the company's directors as well as by its shareholders. However, only shareholders have the right to vote. (It is possible to be a director without being a shareholder, unless a company's articles of association provide otherwise.)

A company's annual general meeting (AGM) is a type of shareholders' meeting. Other shareholders' meetings are known as extraordinary general meetings (EGMs). Twenty-one days' notice is normally required to be provided to the shareholders before an AGM can be validly held, 14 days' notice being required for an EGM. A vote on a proposed resolution is usually taken initially by 'a show of hands'. In the course of such a vote each shareholder (otherwise known as a member of the company) normally has one vote, irrespective of the number of shares s/he possesses. Once the result of the vote on 'a show of hands' is declared, any member may demand what is known as a 'poll' (unless the company's articles specifically provide otherwise).

If a poll is held votes are then counted differently. Rather than each member having one vote regardless of his or her shareholding, each member has one vote for each share s/he holds. The chairman of the company will usually have a casting vote in the event that the number of votes are the same for and against a resolution, in order to enable such a deadlock to be broken. (Article 50 of Table A Articles provides for this for instance.) Shareholders' meetings are usually called by the board. If however the board is reluctant to call a shareholders' meeting then the shareholders can requisition one (as provided by s. 368 CA '85).

TYPES OF RESOLUTIONS

The types of resolutions and their main characteristics are set out below. The first two mentioned are the most common types of resolutions proposed at company meetings.

1. **Ordinary Resolution (OR)** – requires a simple bare majority (i.e. 50% +1 of votes cast) to be passed. Usual notice required to be provided to members of a proposed ordinary resolution is 14 days.

2. **Special Resolution (SR)** – requires 75% of votes cast. Usual notice requirement is 21 days. (Note that this means therefore that if an SR is being proposed at an EGM then the required notice for the EGM will normally be 21 days rather than 14 days.)

3. **Extraordinary Resolution** – similar to a special resolution albeit notice requirement is 14 days (as opposed to 21 days for a special resolution).

4. **Elective Resolution** – enables private companies to 'opt out' of certain company law formalities by unanimous agreement (e.g. to dispense with need to hold an annual general meeting each year).

5. **Written Resolution** – a resolution in writing which can be validly passed without the need for a meeting provided all those entitled to vote sign the written resolution to signify their unanimous approval of the resolution.

HOLDING A SHAREHOLDERS' MEETING

You will recall that in the last chapter you prepared the minutes for the first board meeting of Maplink Limited ('Maplink'). Continuing to act as lawyer for Maplink, you are now asked to prepare the documentation required in order to convene the company's first shareholders' meeting. Remember that the company requires to achieve two specific objectives in the course of that meeting:

■ To appoint Kadir Salleh of 4 Kensington Palace Gardens, London, W2 4AJ (date of birth 4th of April 1969) to the board of directors
■ To change the name of the company from Maplink Limited to Travelgraph Limited.

The steps now required are therefore as follows.

Step 1	Call the first shareholders' meeting
Step 2	Prepare the minutes of the first shareholders' meeting
Step 3	Prepare post-meeting documentation

Exercise 2 – preparing the notice of the meeting

Complete the following notice of the shareholders' meeting (EGM), filling in the blanks by selecting the appropriate words from the list below.

resolutions	convened	passing	vote	Notice
for the purpose of	member	appointed	special	Travelgraph

COMPANY NUMBER 3467609

NOTICE OF EXTRAORDINARY GENERAL MEETING

COMPANIES ACT 1985
COMPANY LIMITED BY SHARES

MAPLINK LIMITED

('The Company')

[1]_____ is hereby given that an extraordinary general meeting of the Company will be held at 44 Princess Diana Walk, South Kensington, London, W2 3SL, on 15 May 2006 at 11.00 a.m. [2]_____ considering and if thought fit [3]_____ the following [4]_____ respectively as ordinary and [5]_____ resolutions of the Company.

▶

23

ORDINARY RESOLUTION

1. That Kadir Salleh be [6]_____ a director of the Company.

SPECIAL RESOLUTION

2. That the name of the Company be changed to [7]_____ Limited

By order of the board

_____

Gisela Wirth

Secretary

Date: 14 April 2006

Registered office: 44 Princess Diana Walk, South Kensington, London, W2 3SL.

Note: A shareholder entitled to attend and vote at the meeting [8]_____ by the notice set out above is entitled to appoint a proxy to attend and [9]_____ in his place. A proxy need not be a [10]_____ of the Company.

Exercise 3 – preparing the minutes

Now complete the following minutes of the company's first shareholders' meeting by deleting each word in bold and writing alongside each deletion in the spaces provided the proper form of those words.

MAPLINK LIMITED

Minutes of an extraordinary general meeting of the Company held at 44 Princess Diana Walk, South Kensington, London, W2 3SL on 15 May 2006 at 11.00 a.m.

Present: Thomas Shapiro

Dimitris Yavaprapas

In Attendance: Gisela Wirth

1. NOTICE AND QUORUM

It was **note**_____ [1] that due notice of the meeting had been given to all members and that a quorum was present. The meeting was therefore **declaration**_____ [2] open.

2. APPOINTMENT OF FURTHER DIRECTOR OF THE COMPANY

The chairman **proposition**_____ [3] the following resolution as an **ordinarily**_____ [4] resolution.
'That Kadir Salleh be appointed a **directorship**_____ [5] of the Company'.
On a show of hands the **chairmanship**_____ [6] declared the resolution passed **unanimity**_____ [7].

3. CHANGE OF COMPANY NAME

The chairman proposed the following resolution as a **specially**_____ [8] resolution:
'That the name of the Company be changed to Travelgraph Limited'.
On a **showing**_____ [9] of hands, the chairman declared the resolution passed unanimously.

CLOSE OF MEETING

There being no further business, the chairman declared the meeting **closure**_____ [10].

_____

Chairman

Exercise 4 – comprehension

Answer the following questions relating to shareholders' meetings.

1. What is meant by a *unanimous agreement*?
2. Name another term meaning the same as *shareholder*.
3. In the text above concerning shareholders' meetings what is meant by a *'deadlock'*?
4. What is a *casting vote*?
5. What does it mean to *requisition* a meeting?
6. Is it illegal to be a director of a company without also being a shareholder of the company?
7. What is the minimum notice period normally required in order to convene an extraordinary general meeting?
8. What minimum notice period will be required to convene the EGM we have considered in this chapter?
9. At the foot of the notice calling the EGM there is a clause intimating that a shareholder is entitled to appoint a *proxy*. What do you think is meant by a proxy?

Exercise 5 – drafting (i)

The following internal memorandum addressed to you from the Head of the Business Law Department sets out the steps now required to complete your client's instructions. Eight prepositions have however been omitted. Fill in these missing prepositions in the numbered blank spaces.

STRINGWOOD & EVANS

Memorandum

From : Jacqueline Hanratty (Head of Business Law Dept.)

To   : [   ]

TRAVELGRAPH LIMITED (FORMERLY MAPLINK LIMITED)

Thank you for doing such a good job [1]＿＿＿＿＿＿ preparing the necessary company documentation for this client company. In order to complete the job we now need to think [2]＿＿＿＿＿＿ the remaining post-meeting matters requiring to be dealt [3]＿＿＿＿＿＿ . In particular, it is now necessary to:

- Update the company's Register of Directors [4]_____ the appointment of Kadir Salleh as a director;
- Notify the Registrar of Companies of Kadir Salleh's appointment to the board [5]_____ completing a Form 288a and forwarding it to the Registrar of Companies within 14 days
- Notify the Registrar of Companies of the change of company name [6]_____ Maplink Limited to Travelgraph Limited by completing and sending a Form NC 20 before the time-limit of 15 days for doing so expires.

The change of company name will not take effect until the Registrar issues an amended Certificate of Incorporation showing the change of name [7]_____ Travelgraph Limited. [8]_____ that date the company will be legally recognised as Travelgraph Limited.

Jacqueline Hanratty

Exercise 6 – post-meeting documentation – drafting (ii)

TASK 1

Complete the following Form 288a (referred to in the above memorandum) to provide notice to the Registrar of Companies of Kadir Salleh's appointment as a director by filling in the shaded spaces.

TASK 2

Similarly complete Form N19 (p. 26) to provide notice to the Registrar of the change of company name by filling in the shaded spaces.

TASK 3

Working in pairs, role-play the board and shareholders' meetings considered in this chapter and the previous one. (One person should play the role of the chairman, Thomas Shapiro, the other person playing the role of the other director, namely Dimitris Yavaprapas.) If you are working in a group then a third person can play the role of Gisela Wirth, the Company Secretary, and make notes on what is discussed at the meeting.

▶

288a

Companies House
for the record

APPOINTMENT of director or secretary
(NOT for resignation (use Form 288b) or change of particulars (use Form 288c))

Please complete in typescript,
or in bold black capitals.

CHWP000

Company Number | 3467609

Company Name in full | MAPLINK LIMITED

	Day	Month	Year		Day	Month	Year	
Date of appointment	1 5 0 5 2 0 0 6			†Date of Birth				[1]

Appointment form

Appointment as director ✓ as secretary ☐ *Please mark the appropriate box. If appointment is as a director and secretary mark both boxes.*

Notes on completion appear on reverse.

NAME *Style / Title | MR.   *Honours etc | LL.B (HONS)

Forename(s) | [2]

Surname | [3]

Previous Forename(s) | NONE   Previous Surname(s) | NONE [4]

†† Tick this box if the address shown is a service address for the beneficiary of a Confidentiality Order granted under the provisions of section 723B of the Companies Act 1985

†† Usual residential address | [4]

Post town | [5]   Postcode | [6]

County / Region | GREATER LONDON   Country | [7]

†Nationality | BRITISH   †Business occupation | ARCHITECT

†Other directorships (additional space overleaf) |

I consent to act as ** director / secretary of the above named company

Consent signature | *Kadir Salleh*   Date | 15th May 2006

* Voluntary details.
† Directors only.
**Delete as appropriate

A director, secretary etc must sign the form below.

Signed | *Gisela Wirth*   Date | 15th May 2006

(**a director / secretary / administrator / administrative receiver / receiver manager / receiver)

You do not have to give any contact information in the box opposite but if you do, it will help Companies House to contact you if there is a query on the form. The contact information that you give will be visible to searchers of the public record..

STRINGWOOD & EVANS,
18 BOND STREET, LONDON
Tel 020 7538 2892

DX number   DX exchange

Companies House receipt date barcode

This form has been provided free of charge by Companies House

Form April 2002

When you have completed and signed the form please send it to the Registrar of Companies at:
Companies House, Crown Way, Cardiff, CF14 3UZ   DX 33050 Cardiff
for companies registered in England and Wales   or
Companies House, 37 Castle Terrace, Edinburgh, EH1 2EB
for companies registered in Scotland   DX 235 Edinburgh
or LP - 4 Edinburgh 2

SPECIAL RESOLUTION ON CHANGE OF NAME
COMPANIES ACTS

COMPANY NUMBER _____ 3467609 _____

COMPANY NAME ▆▆▆▆▆▆▆▆▆▆▆▆▆▆▆▆▆▆▆▆▆▆ [1]

At an [delete as appropriate] Extraordinary General * Meeting of the members of the [2]
above named company, duly convened and held at:

▆▆▆▆▆▆▆▆▆▆▆▆▆▆▆▆▆▆▆▆▆▆ [3]

▆▆▆▆▆▆▆▆▆▆▆▆▆▆▆▆▆▆▆▆▆▆

on the ▆▆▆▆▆▆▆▆ day of ▆▆▆▆▆▆▆▆ 20▆▆ [4]

The following Special Resolution was duly passed:

That the name of the Company be changed to:

NEW NAME ▆▆▆▆▆▆▆▆▆▆▆▆▆▆▆▆▆▆▆▆ [5]

▆▆▆▆▆▆▆▆▆▆▆▆▆▆▆▆▆▆▆▆▆▆

Signature: ___ *Thomas Shapiro* _____
          Chairman, ~~Director, Secretary or Officer~~ of the Company

Notes:

● The resolution must be delivered to Companies House within 15 days of it being passed.

● A £10 fee is required to change the name (cheques made payable to 'Companies House').

● Have you checked whether the new name is available at www.companieshouse.gov.uk ?

● Please provide the name and address to which the certificate is to be sent.

NC 19 (2002)

Law notes

Shareholders' meetings

- Attended by the company's directors and shareholders
- Convened to pass resolutions affecting the constitution of the company (including for instance changes in share capital, approving a director's service contract and changing the name of the company etc.)
- Only shareholders are entitled to vote (including directors who are also shareholders)
- Majority required to pass a resolution depends on the type of resolution being considered

  ordinary resolution (OR) requires 50% + 1 of votes cast

  special resolution (SR) requires 75% of votes cast

Procedure for convening directors' and shareholders' meetings

- Call board (i.e. directors') meeting – any director can call on reasonable notice
- Ensure quorum present and hold board meeting – propose resolutions required, vote on resolutions, adjourn meeting and finalise minutes of meeting
- Call extraordinary general meeting – notice required is normally 14 days or 21 days if SR on agenda
- Ensure quorum present and hold extraordinary general meeting (EGM) – pass resolutions, close meeting and finalise minutes
- 'Present' in the minutes refers to those in attendance and entitled to vote whereas 'In Attendance' refers to those present but with no such right to vote
- Re-convene board meeting – report result of voting on resolutions at EGM and close meeting
- Complete post-meeting documentation

Grammar notes

Prepositions

Many short words in the English language such as *at, in, of* and *after* are prepositions. Prepositions can also however consist of several words, such as *in terms of* and *in the event of*. The only effective way of becoming truly conversant in using prepositions in legal English is through familiarisation with their use in a legal context. Getting into the habit of referring to a good dictionary (such as *Dictionary of Law* by L.B. Curzon) when you are uncertain can also assist in this regard.

As a general rule, prepositions are placed before a noun, as in the following examples:

at court   *the legal proceedings were issued in time*

Alternatively, when used in connection with a phrase containing a noun, a preposition can be placed immediately before such a phrase. Hence:

until further order   *at* the locus

Prepositions can also however come after:

1. a noun–   *Mandy has entered into a <u>contract for</u> service with a large corporation.*

2. an adjective–   *John was <u>delighted with</u> the Judge's decision*

3. a verb–   *How could the Judge possibly <u>arrive at</u> such a decision?*

Lawyers often use formal language. In such circumstances (such as for instance in court) prepositions can be placed before a 'question word' when posing a direct question. For instance:

<u>At</u> what time did you see the accident?

In other formal contexts prepositions can be used immediately before a relative pronoun:

The Defendant is a company with whom the Claimant would like to maintain a business relationship. It is therefore hoped that the negotiated settlement is one <u>from which</u> both parties will benefit.

Use of prepositions to indicate place and time

We can see from this chapter that prepositions are used in relation to company meetings to refer to place and time:

Place:

The shareholders' meeting was held <u>at</u> the company's registered office.

The annual general meeting will be <u>in</u> the main hall.

Time:

The extraordinary general meeting took place <u>at</u> 11.00 a.m.

The next board meeting will be sometime <u>during</u> February

The next meeting must be convened <u>before</u> September.

Geographical variation

Note that there is some degree of variation internationally in the manner in which prepositions are used, particularly in spoken English. For instance, whereas in England it would be common to state *'you have <u>until</u> Wednesday to lodge the document at court',* in the US the word *'through'* is often used in place of *'until'.* Hence in the US you would be more likely to hear *'you have <u>through</u> Wednesday to lodge the document at court'.* It is also common in 'Americanised' English to omit the preposition which would otherwise be placed in a clause immediately before reference to a day in the week. Thus in the US you might hear *'we'll reconvene this meeting first thing Monday',* whereas in England this would be stated as *'we'll reconvene this meeting first thing <u>on</u> Monday'.*

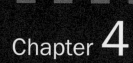

Chapter 4 Boardroom battle!

Learning Objectives

By completing the exercises in this chapter you will:

■ Practice and develop relevant drafting and writing skills within the framework of a boardroom dispute
■ Develop vocabulary relevant to a director's service agreement
■ Acquire knowledge of the practice and procedure involved in removing a director from the board
■ Complete a letter of advice concerning the removal of a director from the board
■ Plan a negotiated settlement of a dispute between directors
■ Negotiate a settlement between parties in dispute within a company
■ Consider the use of relevant grammar including conditional sentences

Removal of a director from the board

The shareholders of a company can remove a director from the board at any time by passing an ordinary resolution (as provided by s. 303 of the Companies Act 1985.) A director can therefore be removed from the board provided over 50% of the votes cast at the shareholders' meeting are in favour of the ordinary resolution to remove the director concerned. That director is entitled to address the meeting with any submissions s/he may wish to make as to why s/he should not be removed from the board.

The 'targeted' director may vote against the ordinary resolution proposing his or her removal provided s/he is also a shareholder. In the course of such a vote the 'targeted' director may have enhanced voting rights (i.e. more than one vote for each share s/he possesses). This will depend on whether the articles of the company contain what is known as a 'Bushell v Faith' clause. Such a clause will typically provide for instance that each share that director holds will carry three votes rather then one when voting takes place on the ordinary resolution seeking his or her removal. The existence of a Bushell v Faith clause in the articles can therefore make it very difficult to remove a director from the board.

Even if a director is removed, s/he may nevertheless have a cause of action against the company for breach of contract. The damages payable by the company in this connection will depend on the terms of any service agreement in existence between the director and the company. This will become clearer as you work through the exercises in this chapter.

Client's instructions

Thomas Shapiro, Managing Director of Travelgraph (formerly Maplink) Limited has come back into your office. He explains that he and his fellow shareholders now regret having appointed Kadir Salleh as a director. Kadir has rarely turned up for work or board meetings. Even when he does he is late.

There have been many arguments between Kadir and the other directors. Last week Kadir shouted at his fellow directors 'Travelgraph's travel guides are rubbish. It's time there were better guides on the market!' Shapiro is particularly annoyed that Kadir is making similar comments to customers and is worried that this is adversely affecting sales. One important customer has already reduced its monthly order. Shapiro also suspects that Kadir is secretly planning to set up his own company in competition with Travelgraph. He now wants your advice on whether Kadir can be removed as a director and if so how.

Exercise 1 – reading and comprehension

The document on p.31 is Kadir Salleh's service agreement with Travelgraph Limited. It is important to consider this carefully before advising Thomas Shapiro further. Read it carefully then answer the following questions, while also citing the specific clause of the service agreement providing the source of your answer. By way of illustration the first question is answered for you.

1. When does Kadir Salleh's service contract commence?   Answer: 10 July 2006 (Clause 2.1)

2. Kadir Salleh's service agreement is a fixed-term agreement. For what period of time?

3. What if any specific duties does Kadir have under the agreement?

4. What is Kadir's annual salary?

5. What if any other benefits is Kadir provided with under the terms of the agreement?

6. Will Kadir be in breach of the service agreement if he does establish his own business in competition to Travelgraph and if so why?

7. Which legal jurisdiction are any disputes between the parties to be resolved under according to the terms of the agreement?

8. Why would a _Bushell_ v _Faith_ clause not assist Kadir Salleh in seeking to prevent his removal from the board?

▶

DIRECTOR'S SERVICE AGREEMENT

THIS AGREEMENT IS MADE ON 10 JULY 2006 BETWEEN:

(1) **TRAVELGRAPH LIMITED ('the Company'),** whose registered office is at 44 Princess Diana Walk, South Kensington, London, W2 3SL

AND

(2) **KADIR SALLEH ('the Sales Director')** of 4 Kensington Palace Gardens, London, W2 4AJ.

IT IS HEREBY AGREED that the aforesaid Kadir Salleh will serve as Sales Director of Travelgraph Limited on the following terms and conditions.

1. DEFINITIONS

In the agreement the following expressions shall have the meanings set out below:

1.1 'the Board'	the board of directors of the Company
1.2 'intellectual property'	trade marks, copyrights, inventions and confidential information

2. TERMS OF ENGAGEMENT

2.1 The Sales Director shall be employed by the Company for an initial fixed-term period of three years commencing from 10 July 2006. This agreement may be terminated thereafter by either party providing to the other not less than six months' notice in writing.

3. DUTIES

3.1 The Sales Director shall during his employment with the Company:
3.1.1. endeavour to promote and develop business on behalf of the Company

4. REMUNERATION

4.1 The Sales Director shall be paid an annual salary of £75,000, payable monthly in arrears on the 28th of each month by direct credit transfer.

5. COMPANY VEHICLE

5.1 The Company shall provide the Sales Director with a Mercedes 300E motorcar and will pay all running costs of said vehicle, including insurance and maintenance.

6. PENSION SCHEME

6.1 The Sales Director will throughout his employment with the Company be eligible to become and remain a member of the Company's pension scheme. The Company will pay into the Company's pension scheme on behalf of the Sales Director an amount equal to 4% of his annual salary during his employment with the Company.

7. HOLIDAY ENTITLEMENT

7.1 The Sales Director shall be entitled to 25 working days' holiday in each calendar year. This is in addition to normal public holidays.

8. CONFIDENTIALITY

8.1 In order to protect the confidentiality of the Company's affairs, business and / or intellectual property rights, the Sales Director hereby agrees not to disclose to any other party during the course of his employment or thereafter any confidential information relating to the Company nor to use any such information in any way for any purpose following termination of employment with the Company. This restriction is to remain valid for a period of 12 months from termination of the Sales Director's employment with the Company.

9. RESTRAINT OF TRADE

9.1 The Sales Director hereby covenants with the Company that he shall not for a period of 12 months following termination of employment with the Company either directly or indirectly engage in or be involved in any activity or business in competition with the Company.

10. LEGAL JURISDICTION

10.1 This agreement shall be governed by English law and the parties hereby submit to the exclusive jurisdiction of the English courts.

Thomas Shapiro

SIGNED BY THOMAS SHAPIRO

For and on behalf of Travelgraph Limited

Kadir Salleh

SIGNED BY KADIR SALLEH

Of 4 Kensington Palace Gardens, London, W2 4AJ

Dated this 10th day of July 2006.

Exercise 2 – vocabulary (i)

Unscramble the following, re-writing the words (which are all contained in the above agreement) by placing the letters in the correct order. By way of illustration the first one is done for you.

1. civseer naeetregm	s e r v i c e a g r e e m e n t
2. merts dan tidinsoonc	t _ _ _ _ _ _ _ c _ _ _ _ _ _ _ _
3. tinidisfeon	_ _ _ _ _ _ _ _ _ _

▶

4. tonymempel	_ _ _ _ _ _ _ _ _ _
5. nuirtonemare	_ _ _ _ _ _ _ _ _ _ _
6. telnettiemn	e _ _ _ _ _ _ _ _ _ _
7. cityfitinonadel	c _ _ _ _ _ _ _ _ _ _ _ _ _
8. lucenetaillt retropyp	i _ _ _ _ _ _ _ _ _ _ _ p _ _ _ _ _ _ _
9. startiner fo dater	r _ _ _ _ _ _ _ _ o _ t _ _ _ _
10. sirijconduit	_ _ _ _ _ _ _ _ _ _ _

Exercise 3 – letter writing

The following document is a draft letter of advice to Thomas Shapiro addressing his instructions. It contains a number of omissions. Complete the letter by filling in the blank spaces with appropriate words. (The necessary information to complete this exercise can be found from the information already provided.)

STRINGWOOD & EVANS
18 BOND STREET
LONDON
W1 1KR

▐ + 44 020 7538 2892

10 January 2007

T. Shapiro Esq.
Travelgraph Limited
44 Princess Diana Walk
South Kensington
London
W2 3SL

Dear Mr Shapiro,

Re. Removal of Kadir Salleh from the Board of Travelgraph Limited

I now write to advise you on the legal position concerning your wish to remove Mr Salleh from the board.

Procedure for Removal

[1]_____ of the Companies Act 1985 (CA) enables the [2]_____ of a company to remove a [3]_____ from office. The procedure required is basically as follows.

An ordinary [4]_____ will have to be passed by the shareholders, requiring a simple [5]_____ (i.e. over 50 % of the votes cast). This criterion does not appear to present a problem since Mr Salleh does not hold any [6]_____ in the company despite being a director. He does not therefore personally possess any voting power with which to oppose the [7]_____ proposing his removal.

In addition, your personal [8]_____ amounts to 70% of the company's authorised and issued share capital. This means you control over 50% of the votes available. You are therefore able to [9]_____ the required [10]_____ resolution regardless of whether the other shareholders [11]_____ for or against the resolution.

Mr Salleh does however have the right to have any written [12]_____ he may wish to make in his defence distributed to the [13]_____ prior to the resolution being [14]_____ upon. Twenty-one days [15]_____ is required of the shareholders' [16]_____ at which the resolution will be proposed.

Possible Consequences of Removal

I have reviewed the copy of Mr Salleh's service [17]_____ . It is important to appreciate that this is a three year [18]_____ - _____ contract and that two and a half years of this term remains unexpired. While therefore it will be possible to [19]_____ Mr Salleh from the board by [20]_____ resolution as set out above, this is likely to prove expensive to the company. In particular, Mr Salleh will have a meritorious claim for [21]_____ on the basis of [22]_____ of _____ . In addition, there is a six months' [23]_____ provision upon culmination of the three-year period. He will therefore be able to claim damages for monies remaining payable under the agreement (i.e. three years' earnings). With a view to seeking to minimise the cost of Mr Kadir's [24]_____ from the board I would be pleased to assist you in [25]_____ a mutually beneficial [26]_____ . I look forward to receiving your further instructions.

Yours sincerely,

Exercise 4 – vocabulary (ii)

Select from the letter of advice you have now completed alternative words or phrases similar in meaning to each of the following.

1. members of a company	s _ _ _ _ _ _ _ _ _ _ _
2. amount of shares a person possesses	s _ _ _ _ _ _ _ _ _ _ _
3. submissions	r _ _ _ _ _ _ _ _ _ _ _ _ _
4. gathering of shareholders	s _ _ _ _ _ _ _ _ _ _ _ m _ _ _ _ _ _
5. resolution passed by simple majority	o _ _ _ _ _ _ _ r _ _ _ _ _ _ _ _ _
6. contract for a specific period of time	f _ _ _ _ - t _ _ _ c _ _ _ _ _ _ _

Exercise 5 – composition

The first parts of complete sentences are listed in the first column below. Complete each of these sentences by matching each of these parts with its corresponding part in the second column. By way of illustration the first one is done for you.

1. If a settlement is reached this will result in —————— by English law
2. A carefully drafted confidentiality clause   per s. 303 Companies Act 1985
3. Kadir Salleh's service contract is governed by   another agreement!
4. Removing a director will not prevent   can protect a company's trade secrets
5. Shareholders can remove a director by ordinary resolution   a breach of contract claim

Exercise 6 – role-play (i)

ADVISING YOUR CLIENT

In pairs, role-play a meeting between Thomas Shapiro and his lawyer for the purpose of providing Thomas Shapiro with advice on the law and procedure involved in removing Kadir Salleh from the board. One of you should play the role of the client (Thomas Shapiro) and the other the role of the lawyer. The person role-playing the client should be prepared to ask relevant questions. The person playing the lawyer's role should be prepared to provide relevant advice. If you are working on your own then imagine that you are the lawyer about to meet with Thomas Shapiro and make notes of the advice you would provide at the meeting.

Exercise 7 – role-play (ii)

NEGOTIATION

An ordinary resolution has now been passed to remove Kadir Salleh from the board of directors. In response, Kadir has appointed a firm of lawyers to represent his interests. This firm has sent a letter of claim to Travelgraph Limited intimating that they intend to issue legal proceedings on Kadir's behalf for breach of contract unless satisfactory proposals for payment of compensation are made by Travelgraph forthwith. A meeting for a 'without prejudice' discussion between the parties has therefore been scheduled to take place at Stringwood & Evans' office tomorrow morning.

Task 1

Prepare to negotiate at the meeting on behalf of Travelgraph Limited by completing the negotiation plan on the next page. When preparing this plan you should take into account the information already provided in this chapter.

NEGOTIATION PLAN

Before engaging in negotiation on behalf of your client consider the following:

A. The client's aims / goals. Set out below the client's main aims / goals.

B. The opponent's likely aims / goals. Set out below what you anticipate these will be.

C. Specific strengths in your client's case. Identify one example.

D. Specific strengths in your opponent's case. Identify one example.

E. Specific weaknesses in your client's case. Identify one example.

F. Specific weaknesses in your opponent's case. Identify one example.

G. Your strategy for achieving your client's objectives. For instance are you going to make an opening offer or wait for the other party to make an offer? What is your opening offer going to be or your response to the other party's opening offer? What is the maximum amount you are prepared to offer? What concessions are you prepared to make in order to achieve a settlement (e.g. will you offer a reference? Or perhaps let the other party keep the company car?). Set out these details below.

▶

Task 2

In pairs, now try role-playing the negotiation between Travelgraph's lawyer and Kadir Salleh's lawyer. One of you should play the role of Travelgraph's lawyer and the other the role of Kadir Salleh's lawyer. Decide between yourselves which role each person will play, then follow the further instructions below. [If you are working on your own then imagine you are the lawyer for Telegraph Ltd and about to meet Kadir Salleh's lawyer to try to negotiate a settlement. Prepare notes in readiness for the meeting, setting out details of what you intend to say and of what questions you would ask Kadir's lawyer. Read the section below headed 'Further information for Travelgraph Limited's representative', and take account of this further information.]

Further instructions

IF YOU ARE ACTING FOR TRAVELGRAPH LIMITED:

Read the further details below relating to your client (headed 'Further Information for Travelgraph Limited's Representative') before commencing the negotiation.

IF YOU ARE ACTING FOR KADIR SALLEH:

Read the further details below relating to your client (headed 'Further Information for Kadir Salleh's Representative') before commencing the negotiation.

DO NOT READ THE FURTHER DETAILS RELATING TO THE OTHER PARTY BEFORE CONDUCTING THIS EXERCISE – REGARD THE OTHER PARTY'S FURTHER INFORMATION AS PRIVILEGED INFORMATION BETWEEN THAT PARTY AND HIS/HER LAWYER.

Now try role-playing the negotiation, endeavouring to reach a mutually beneficial settlement agreement. (You should assume that the date of the negotiation is 11 January 2007.) Take written notes of the terms of any agreement you reach with your opponent. Compare these notes with your opponent's notes when you have completed the negotiation, checking that you have both accurately recorded the same details of what has been agreed!

Task 3

Choose another colleague to play the role of your client. Report back orally to this colleague on the outcome of the negotiation, relating clearly the details of the agreement or outcome of the negotiation.

Task 4

Fill in the 'Negotiation Feedback Form' at the end of this chapter. Finally, taking account of the answers you have provided on this form, discuss constructively with your opponent in the negotiation your thoughts and opinions about both your own and your opponent's negotiating performance. (You will find this feedback exercise helpful in enhancing your skill and effectiveness in planning and conducting future negotiations.)

FURTHER INFORMATION FOR KADIR SALLEH'S
REPRESENTATIVE

Kadir Salleh is in financial difficulties and is anxious to reach an agreement rather than incur the time and cost of court action. He is however prepared to pursue litigation if a reasonable settlement cannot be achieved. Kadir has been in discussion with a competitor since he has felt insecure for some time at Travelgraph, the other directors having been unfriendly to him recently. He has not as yet made any firm commitment to join any other company. He accepts that his work performance has been poor recently due to his financial worries (caused by recent heavy gambling in London casinos). He is therefore prepared to compromise over the amount of compensation he will settle for. He is insistent however that the company provides him with a favourable reference, this being important to him in seeking alternative employment. He would be prepared to sign a confidentiality clause if Travelgraph insists on this as a term of settlement.

▶

FURTHER INFORMATION FOR TRAVELGRAPH LIMITED'S REPRESENTATIVE

The board is anxious to reach an amicable settlement if possible in order to avoid protracted proceedings in court. In addition to the potential expense of such proceedings, the board is concerned that a court case will attract unfavourable publicity which would adversely affect the company's reputation and sales. Travelgraph's profit forecast is poor for the coming year. The shareholders believe that Kadir Salleh is at least to some extent to blame for this. The company is not therefore prepared to offer compensation amounting to three years' earnings. It will nevertheless offer a reasonable amount, the board being keen to avoid a court case if at all possible for the reasons set out above. The company would however require a confidentiality clause to be included in any agreement reached, prohibiting Salleh from publicly disclosing the terms of the settlement. The company would be prepared to provide a favourable reference if this concession resulted in a satisfactory resolution of the whole matter.

NEGOTIATION FEEDBACK FORM

1. On a scale of 1 to 10, how successful do you think you were overall in achieving your client's objectives?

2. On a scale of 1 to 10, how successful do you think your opponent was in achieving his / her client's objectives?

3. Tick the appropriate box to indicate your opinion on how successful you were regarding the outcome as far as monetary compensation was concerned:

   a) no specific amount of monetary compensation was agreed upon ☐

   b) the amount agreed upon was far higher than I anticipated would be agreed ☐

   c) the amount agreed upon was slightly higher than I anticipated would be agreed ☐

   d) the amount agreed upon was very close to the amount I anticipated would be agreed ☐

   e) the amount agreed upon was slightly lower than the amount I anticipated would be agreed ☐

   f) the amount agreed upon was much lower than the amount I anticipated would be agreed ☐

4. How would you describe your opponent's attitude to you in the course of the negotiation. (For instance was it conciliatory or aggressive etc.?)

5. Which argument did you put forward which proved to be the most effective / persuasive and why?

6. Which argument did your opponent put forward which proved to be the most effective / persuasive and why?

7. In what way (if any) would you plan and / or negotiate differently next time?

Law notes

Removal of a director

- A director can be removed by passing an ordinary resolution (OR) at a shareholders' meeting, per s. 303 Companies Act 1985 (CA '85)
- Requires simple majority (i.e. over 50% of votes cast) in favour
- Special notice of OR required (i.e. 21 days), per s. 303(2) and s. 379 CA '85
- Director concerned is entitled to address the meeting
- If director concerned is also a shareholder then articles of company may provide for 'weighted' voting rights, i.e. a *Bushell* v *Faith* clause
- Shareholders' power to remove a director under s. 303 CA '85 does not deprive director concerned of right to claim damages for breach of contract
- Articles of a company can also provide for a director becoming disqualified from continuing as a director in specific circumstances (e.g. upon bankruptcy)
- Any service contract provided to a director for over five years' duration requires approval by shareholders (s. 319 CA '85)

Grammar notes

Conditional sentences

Conditional sentences are commonly used when negotiating a settlement. For example:

If you pay within 14 days Mr Salleh will accept £100,000 in full and final settlement.

Note that in the first part of this structure we have 'if' and present tense followed by 'will' in the second clause. In this way the person making the settlement offer (the *offeror*) can make it clear that the settlement being proposed is subject to a condition. (I.e. that payment is made within 14 days.)

Conditional sentences can similarly be used to issue a warning. For instance:

If you do not accept this offer we will proceed to court.

The word *should* is commonly used in a professional context with this future form of conditional sentence in place of *if*. This conveys a more reserved and formal impression to the reader or listener. Thus:

Should you encounter any further difficulties in the future please inform me.

The word *should* is also used in a professional context in place of the word *would* in other present or future forms of conditional sentences. Thus:

I should also make clear that this offer is conditional upon early acceptance.

Conditional sentences can also be used in a more hypothetical form which is also encountered in legal negotiations. This involves the use of the word *were* followed by the infinitive with 'to'. Thus:

▶

If we were to make an offer there would have to be some assurance that this would be kept secret.

It is also possible to invert *were* along with the subject and to omit *if*. Thus:

Were we to make an offer there would have to be some assurance that this would be kept secret.

Legal English also uses conjunctions in conditional sentences, such as:

until; although; provided that; unless; in order that; on condition that etc.

E.g. *We wouldn't make an offer <u>unless</u> there was an assurance that this would be kept secret.*

Modal verbs (such as *may, can, could, should* and *ought to*) can also be used where a possibility rather than a certainty is being discussed. Thus:

If you can assure us this will remain confidential we <u>may</u> put forward an offer.

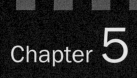

Chapter 5   Marketing agreements

Learning Objectives

By completing the exercises in this chapter you will:

- Analyse a marketing agreement, taking account of a client's instructions
- Consider different types of marketing agreements
- Amend a marketing agreement in accordance with a client's instructions
- Develop vocabulary relevant to marketing agreements
- Develop grammatical and written word skills relevant to drafting legal documentation
- Become familiar with realistic legal precedents and how to use them for drafting
- Acquire practice in drafting commercial documentation and achieving clarity of meaning in your drafting

Introduction

There are various types of marketing agreements including:

- Agency agreements
- Distribution agreements
- Franchising agreements
- Joint venture agreements

Agency agreement

A traditional sales agency agreement is an agreement whereby a company (known as the principal) authorises another company or individual (known as the agent) to sell the principal's goods on its behalf. The agent thus sells the goods on behalf of the principal (rather than purchase the goods itself). When a customer purchases from the agent the contractual relationship (known as 'privity of contract') will thereby legally exist directly between the principal and the purchaser (the agent receiving commission on such sales).

Distribution agreement

This is an agreement whereby a company (termed the supplier) actually sells its goods to another company (the distributor). When the distributor then sells the goods on to its own customer there is no contract created between the supplier and the final customer (the contract being between the distributor and its customer). The distributor therefore receives no commission from the supplier, instead earning profit from the 'mark-up' between the price it paid the supplier and the price it sold the goods on for. (Distribution agreements must be drafted very carefully since many agreements which restrict competition and therefore consumer choice are now illegal under European Community law.)

Franchise agreement

A company (the franchisor) can expand its business nationally and internationally by entering into franchise agreements with other parties (known as franchisees). This is known as franchising a business. Franchising is appropriate to businesses with an established brand. A franchise agreement imposes requirements on the franchisee to operate the business in accordance with a uniform business model (for instance by stipulating the colour scheme and interior layout of the franchisee's premises). The franchisee benefits however by being associated with a well recognised brand-name. Many well-known high street brands are franchises, such as fast-food restaurants.

Joint venture agreement

This is an arrangement in which two or more businesses agree to co-operate or in other words 'join forces' on a particular business venture or project. This enables companies to undertake initiatives which they may not have the resources to undertake individually, sharing risks while also combining their financial and skills resources. Care is again required in drafting joint venture agreements in order to avoid contravening European Community law competition rules and/or US competition law (known as 'anti-trust' law).

Exercise 1 – comprehension

TASK 1

Answer true or false to each of the following questions based on the text above.

1. An agent purchases goods directly from a principal.
2. Under an agency agreement a contract exists between the principal and ultimate customer.
3. Under a distribution agreement the distributor purchases goods directly from a supplier.
4. An entirely unknown company would usually be a suitable business to franchise.

TASK 2

Answer the following questions.

1. Name one company or brand-name you can think of which is a franchise.
2. What is an agent's income from sales known as?
3. How does a distributor earn income on sales?
4. State one benefit to a company of entering into a joint venture agreement.

■ Drafting agreements

Drafting is an important skill for a lawyer. Drafting in the legal sense means to compose legal documentation (including for instance legal correspondence, court orders, contracts and legislation). Precision is essential when drafting legal agreements; otherwise there may be scope for ambiguity in the course of interpreting the intended meaning of the terms of the agreement. This in turn can lead to subsequent dispute between the parties to the agreement. Drafting practice provides the opportunity to develop your skill in the use of legal English.

Exercise 2 – document completion

The following agreement relates to the appointment of an agent by an aircraft manufacturer called Cadmium Aerospace Limited. Complete this sales agency agreement on behalf of Cadmium Aerospace Limited by selecting the appropriate word to enter in each blank space from the alternatives in brackets.

AGENCY AGREEMENT

THIS AGREEMENT is made on the 19th day of July 2007

BETWEEN:

(1) CADMIUM AEROSPACE LIMITED, whose registered office is at 168 Hanover Square, London, W1 ('the Principal')

AND

(2) MACFADYEN AVIATION LIMITED, whose registered office is at 115 Duxford Road, Cambridge, CM3 ('the Agent').

---

1. APPOINTMENT

The Principal [1] _____ [hereby / thus / thereafter] appoints the Agent and the Agent agrees to act as the Agent of the Principal for the purpose of promoting and selling the Principal's aircraft throughout Europe and North America ('the Territory'). It is [2] _____ [nevertheless / whereby / further] agreed that this agreement shall be valid for a period of two years. [3] _____ [Hereunder / Moreover / Whereby] the Principal agrees not to appoint any other agent in the territory and [4] _____ [hereof / conversely / furthermore] agrees not to seek nor enter into sales itself within the Territory during the period of the Agreement.

2. AGENT'S OBLIGATIONS

2.1 The Agent [5] _____ [hereunder / hereof / hereby] undertakes to use its best endeavours to market and achieve sales of the Principal's aircraft in the Territory. The Agent is also [6] _____ [henceforth / subsequently / hereinafter] authorised to enter into contracts for the sale of the Principal's aircraft for and on behalf of the Principal.

2.2 [7] _____ [Herein / Alternatively / In addition], the Agent undertakes to provide the Principal with market reports on monthly sales and competitors' activities.

2.3 The Agent shall make appropriate credit checks on potential customers in order to ensure their credit-worthiness.

3. PRINCIPAL'S OBLIGATIONS

3.1 The Principal hereby agrees that [8] _____ [hereto / during / meanwhile] the continuance of the Agreement it will:

3.1.1 provide the Agent with training on the Principal's aircraft;

3.1.2 provide customers with technical and servicing report;

3.1.3 provide the Agent with marketing and publicity material to assist the Agent with marketing the Principal's aircraft [9] _____ [within / nevertheless / hereafter] the Territory.

4. REMUNERATION

4.1 The Agent shall receive from the Principal in consideration of its services hereunder commission as follows:

4.1.1 at a rate of 5% of the Net Selling Price for each single engined 'Strato-Line' airplane sold;

4.1.2 at a rate of 7% of the Net Selling Price for each twin engined 'Skymaster' airplane sold.

EXECUTED BY _____ (Sales Director)

For and on behalf of CADMIUM AEROSPACE LIMITED

EXECUTED BY _____ (Chief Executive Officer)

For and on behalf of MACFADYEN AVIATION LIMITED

Exercise 3 – sentence structure

TASK 1

Cadmium Aerospace has now notified you that it wishes to include a further clause in the agreement providing either party with the right to terminate the agreement at any time with three months' notice. Re-arrange the following clauses in the correct order to produce an appropriate sentence which fulfils this purpose.

This agreement shall continue in force / three calendar months notice in writing / be terminated by either party providing to the other / for a period of two years save and except that it may

TASK 2

It has now been agreed between the two parties to the agreement that Cadmium Aerospace may terminate the agreement at the end of the first year in the event that MacFadyen Aviation Limited does not achieve sales of at least £750,000 by that time. Re-arrange the following clauses in the correct order to produce an appropriate sentence which fulfils this purpose.

£750,000 within / the Principal shall be entitled / by notifying the Agent in writing accordingly / In the event that / to terminate this Agreement / the Agent fails to achieve a minimum total sales amount of / twelve months of the commencement of this Agreement

Exercise 4 – drafting

The parties to the agreement have further agreed that the agent is to receive a bonus in addition to the commission already agreed if the agent achieves sales exceeding £1,250,000 by the end of the first year of the agency agreement. This bonus will be 1% of total net sales made by the agent within this first year of the agreement.

(a) Draft a suitable clause which complies with these further instructions.
(b) Which paragraph number would be a suitable place to locate this additional clause within the agreement?

NOTE TO READERS WORKING IN A GROUP: Compare your draft of the clause in Exercise 4(a) above with a colleague. Consider which draft is clearest, structured best and best meets the client's wishes. Then try to agree a final version of the clause between you. Write out this re-drafted clause. You can then present this re-drafted clause to the rest of your group for constructive discussion and feedback on clarity of meaning.

NOTE TO READERS WORKING INDIVIDUALLY: Re-read your draft of the clause in Exercise 4(a) above. Be critical of your draft, considering how you could possibly improve the structure and content. E.g. could you make your sentences shorter? Is your wording clear in meaning? Does it fully set out what your client intends?

Interviewing and advising

Interviewing is an important means of communication between a lawyer and client. Effective interviewing involves a combination of general skills including those of listening, questioning, note taking, fact gathering and assimilation. Many complaints by clients against their lawyers relate to insufficient communication. Competence in interviewing and advising is therefore a prerequisite to proper client care.

A properly conducted interview usually involves the following stages:

Interviewing and Advising Checklist

1. INTRODUCTION

Set the client at ease initially, exchanging 'pleasantries' and establishing a good rapport with the client. (Sometimes known as the 'meet, greet and seat' stage.)

2. INFORMATION GATHERING

At this stage the lawyer invites the client to explain his/her problems and concerns with a view to ascertaining the client's aims and goals. This is primarily a listening stage.

3. ADVISING

At this stage the lawyer provides advice, addressing the client's specific questions and concerns. This advice should be explained clearly and accurately.

4. CONCLUSION

At this juncture the lawyer should ensure that the client understands clearly what has been discussed and the advice which has been provided. This can often be achieved by the lawyer providing a short 'recap' of his/her advice.

Exercise 5 – interviewing and advising

TASK 1

Read the following memorandum from your secretary at Stringwood & Evans.

STRINGWOOD & EVANS

Solicitors

Client: Cadmium Aerospace Limited   Date: 30 July 2007

File Reference: CA 001

Matter: Agency Agreement with MacFadyen Aviation Ltd.

The Sales Director of Cadmium Aerospace Limited, Frederick Johannsen, telephoned this afternoon. I have made an appointment for him to see you in your office tomorrow morning at 11.00 a.m. He wants to discuss the above mentioned agency agreement with you. In particular, he wants you to advise him concerning:

■ Whether Cadmium Aerospace can appoint other agents within Europe and North America during the course of the agency agreement
■ Whether the Principal can sell directly to customers within Europe and North America as well as through MacFadyen Aviation Ltd while the agreement remains in force
■ Details of how the Principal is required under the agreement to assist the agent to achieve sales
■ An explanation of how the agent's commission is to be calculated in accordance with the agreement.

Regards,

Tracey

TASK 2

If you are working in a group then undertake the 'Group exercise' below.
If you are working on your own then undertake the 'Individual exercise' below.

Group exercise

Role-play the interview with Frederick Johannsen as follows. Pair up with a colleague. One of you should play the role of the client, Frederick Johannsen, the other person playing the role of the lawyer. The client should explain to the lawyer the matters he seeks advice on, based on the information in the memorandum above. Take notes of the advice provided. The lawyer should provide advice to the client, addressing the matters set out in the memorandum above (taking account of the 'Interviewing and Advising Checklist'). Refer to the relevant ▶

sections of the agency agreement in support of your advice. Take notes of the information the client provides and of the questions the client asks, along with notes of the advice you provide.

Finally, provide feedback to your partner on his/her performance in interviewing and advising by grading him/her under each of the four criteria in the 'Interview and Advising Checklist'. Grade from 1 to 5 as follows: 1 = unsatisfactory; 2 = poor; 3 = average; 4 = very good; 5 = outstanding. Ask your partner to similarly provide feedback to you on your performance.

Individual exercise

Firstly imagine that you are the client, Frederick Johannsen. Prepare a list of questions to ask the lawyer advising you which address the matters of concern to you as set out in the memorandum above.

Then assume that you are the lawyer providing advice to Frederick Johannsen. Prepare for the interview with your client by writing out a brief summary of your advice regarding the four questions raised in the memorandum from your secretary. (Include in your summary the relevant paragraph numbers of the agreement which support your answer.)

Law notes

Marketing agreements

Agency agreement
- Agent sells goods or services on behalf of a principal, the principal selling directly to the final customer
- Privity of contract exists between the principal and the ultimate purchaser
- Agent receives commission
- Agency agreements are often more suitable for high-value items such as aero-engines etc.
- Agent's duties include:
  1. promoting the goods or services in the market place
  2. providing principal with feedback information on sales and market trends
  3. maintaining confidentiality regarding principal's trade secrets
- Principal's duties involve acting in good faith towards the agent and usually include:
  1. paying commission
  2. supplying advertising and promotional literature
  3. supplying stock as required and after-sales service

Distribution agreement
- Supplier sells to a distributor in a particular market (often in another country), no contract existing between the supplier and the final customer
- Distributor earns income from 'mark-up' between price paid to supplier for goods and selling price to customer

■ Distributor's duties usually include:
1. purchasing a specified minimum amount of stock from the supplier on a regular basis
2. marketing and promoting effectively goods purchased from the supplier and keeping supplier informed of sales levels and market trends
3. ensuring that similar competitors' products are not sold or promoted (albeit care has to be taken not to contravene European competition law rules relating to restriction on competition in this respect)

■ Supplier's duties usually include:
1. providing advertising and sales promotional material
2. selling a specified amount of stock regularly to the distributor
3. indemnifying the distributor from any legal liability resulting from any defect in the products

Franchising agreement

A contractual arrangement in which a *franchisor* appoints a *franchisee* to operate as a separate business offering the franchisor's goods or services. The franchisee usually pays a *franchise fee* as well as possibly a continuing royalty fee on sales. In return the franchisee benefits from a recognised 'brand-image'.

Joint venture agreement

An agreement whereby two or more separate businesses co-operate with each other on a particular commercial venture or project. Such an agreement enables the separate businesses to combine resources and to share financial risk for mutual benefit.

Grammar notes

Points to remember when drafting legal documents

Active or passive voice

Use the active voice rather than the passive when drafting legal documents. (Use of the passive can result in longer clauses as well as ambiguity.) The object of the active verb becomes the subject in the passive.

E.g. 'The contract was drawn up by the solicitor' is a passive sentence. This could be re-written as follows to make it active: 'The solicitor drew up the contract.'

Remember however that the passive voice is appropriate in the following circumstances:

■ When the emphasis and purpose of the sentence is primarily to notify the act as opposed to the person performing it. E.g. 'Legal proceedings were served yesterday';
■ When the identity of the individual conducting the act is irrelevant and/or anonymous. E.g. 'The vehicle was wrecked';
■ When it is intended that the identity of the person conducting the act should remain anonymous (for instance in order to prevent blame being attributed to a particular person). E.g. 'There was negligence'.

▶

Grammar and punctuation

Try to avoid using more words than necessary. For example, instead of 'by means of' the word 'by' is usually sufficient. Similarly, rather than 'on a monthly basis' use 'monthly'. Avoid separating the subject and the verb and similarly the verb and the object.

E.g. 'This agreement, unless termination has transpired on a prior date, shall terminate on 17 October 2007.'

Consider instead:

'Unless earlier revoked, the agreement shall terminate on 17 October 2007.'

Correct punctuation is also important to clarify the intended meaning. Thus ensure full-stops are placed correctly to signify the end of each sentence. Also use commas to signify appropriate pauses (similar to those you would make when speaking). Commas should also normally be used at the start of a quotation. E.g., *The witness said, 'I did not see the other vehicle'*. In addition, if using commas instead of brackets then remember to place both commas in the appropriate part of the sentence.

E.g. 'The law accepts, as a matter of course, that damages are recoverable for negligence.'

Be careful however to use commas appropriately. Incorrect use can result in inaccuracy of meaning. Similarly consider whether other punctuation marks are appropriate, such as:

■ The semi-colon (;) – which can fulfil a similar function to a full-stop, enabling for instance two closely related points to be included in one sentence.
■ The colon (:) – which can be used as the prelude to a list (such as bullet points) or prior to citing a quotation.
■ The apostrophe (') – to indicate 'possession' or omission of a letter (e.g. 'doesn't' instead of 'does not'). Note however that such informal abbreviation of words will not usually be appropriate for formal legal documents.
■ The question mark (?) – place at the end of a directly posed question. E.g. 'Did you see the silver Ford motor car before it struck your vehicle?'

Vocabulary

It is fairly common in legal English for adverbs to be placed at the beginning of a sentence as a means of connecting the sentence to the rest of the text. You have come across some of these in the course of considering the legal documentation in this chapter. There are a number of such sentence adverbs and adverbials which will assist you in writing clear legal English, including the following expressions.

Accordingly	Hereinafter	Meanwhile
Alternatively	Hereinbefore	Moreover
As a result	Hereof	Nevertheless
As a whole	Hereunder	Nonetheless
Clearly	However	On the contrary
Coincidentally	In addition	Overall
Conversely	In all the circumstances	Primarily
Equally	In any event	Secondly
Finally	In conclusion	Significantly
Fundamentally	In consequence thereof	Similarly
Furthermore	In contrast	Subsequently
Further or alternatively	In essence	Therefore
Henceforth	In particular	Thereto
Hereby	In so far as	Thus
Herein	In summary	Whereby

PART 2

Civil litigation

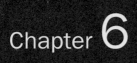

Chapter 6 Injunctions

Learning Objectives

By completing the exercises in this chapter you will be able to:

■ Determine appropriate terms and vocabulary for an injunction order in compliance with your client's instructions
■ Consider appropriate grammar including modal verbs and tenses
■ Appreciate the legal aspects of an injunction order
■ Consider and understand the effect of a prohibitory injunction order
■ Consider and draft a prohibitory injunction order on behalf of a client

Introduction

An injunction is a court order requiring a party to do (or prohibiting a party from doing) a particular act. Some injunctions are required extremely urgently if they are to be effective. There is also sometimes a need to obtain an injunction in secrecy. This need will arise where giving notice of the application to the party the injunction is being sought against would be likely to defeat the purpose of obtaining the injunction. In such situations the injunction application can be made to court without providing notice of the application to that other party.

Drafting injunction orders

When applying for an injunction order it is usual practice to draft the order you are asking the court to grant. This draft order can then be produced to the Judge to indicate the terms of the injunction order you are seeking on behalf of your client. We shall draft such an order shortly, but first let us consider a few 'good practice' points for drafting injunction orders.

Exercise 1 – reading

GOOD PRACTICE GUIDANCE FOR DRAFTING INJUNCTION ORDERS

The wording of an injunction order requires careful thought. It is necessary to state clearly and precisely what the party the order is being made against (termed the 'Respondent') may do, must do and/or must not do. There must not therefore be any uncertainty as to the meaning of the terms of the injunction.

If there is any ambiguity in your description of what the Respondent is being prohibited from or compelled to do then this may provide the Respondent with a legal 'loophole'. This could defeat the intended purpose of the injunction. (For example, by enabling the Respondent to continue doing something which the injunction was specifically intended to prevent the Respondent from doing.) That is why it is crucial that the terms you draft are sufficiently precise in meaning to ensure that the injunction is legally 'watertight'.

Nowadays the court expects the draft order to be written in plain English rather than archaic legal language or 'jargon'. Often the Respondent being served with an injunction will be an individual who is not a lawyer. The terms setting out what he or she is being ordered by the court to do or not to do must therefore be readily understandable by a layperson (particularly since failure to comply with an injunction results in the defaulting party being in contempt of court).

Facts pattern

You are now a partner in the law firm named Stringwood & Evans, located at 18 Bond Street, London, W1 1KR (telephone number 020 7538 2892). Thomas Shapiro, Managing Director of Travelgraph Limited, has consulted you. (This is the same client who provides you with instructions in Chapters 1 to 4 of the Business Law and Practice Section.) Thomas Shapiro explains that Kadir Salleh, a former director of Travelgraph, left the company last month. Shapiro and his fellow directors at Travelgraph are very concerned however because Kadir Salleh is about to join a competitor called Worldlink Limited.

Worldlink Limited is a major competitor of Travelgraph, their premises also being in the city (only a few miles away in fact from Travelgraph's office at 44 Princess Diana Walk, South Kensington, London, W2 3SL). Thomas Shapiro has also discovered that Worldlink Limited intend to publish a new series of travel guides of major world cities using computer files belonging to Travelgraph. Kadir Salleh had access to these files in the course of his previous employment with Travelgraph. Thomas Shapiro is furious to now learn that Salleh has retained possession of these and that he has disclosed all this confidential material and information to Worldlink Limited.

Thomas Shapiro shows you a page from Kadir Salleh's service agreement with Travelgraph, indicating valid restrictive covenants preventing Kadir Salleh for a period of 12 months from:

■ Working for a competitor

- Disclosing confidential information acquired by him in the course of his employment with Travelgraph (including computer files) to Worldlink Limited or any other party

Thomas Shapiro now therefore wants you to obtain an injunction on behalf of Travelgraph Limited against Kadir Salleh to enforce these terms, thereby preventing Salleh from:

- Commencing work with Worldlink Limited
- Disclosing confidential information (including computer files acquired by him in the course of working for Travelgraph Limited) to Worldlink Limited or any other party

Assume that this application will be presented to the High Court in London tomorrow (25 February 2007). Now read the following relevant excerpt from Kadir Salleh's service agreement with Travelgraph Limited which Thomas Shapiro has handed to you.

EXTRACT FROM KADIR SALLEH'S SERVICE AGREEMENT WITH TRAVELGRAPH LIMITED

CONFIDENTIALITY

In order to protect the confidentiality of the Company's affairs, business and/or intellectual property rights, the Sales Director hereby agrees not to disclose to any other party during the course of his employment or thereafter any confidential information (including in electronic form) relating to the Company nor to use any such information in any way for any purpose following termination of employment with the Company. This restriction is to remain valid for a period of 12 months from termination of the Sales Director's employment with the Company.

RESTRAINT OF TRADE

The Sales Director hereby covenants with the Company that he shall not for a period of 12 months following termination of employment with the Company either directly or indirectly engage in, be involved in or employed by any activity or business in competition with the Company.

Exercise 2 – drafting

The following is a precedent for a suitable type of injunction order. Complete the drafting of the injunction to comply with your client's instructions by:

1. deleting clauses in square brackets within the draft as appropriate
2. completing the blank spaces using relevant information from the text above as well as by selecting appropriate entries from the following panel ▶

Phrases for inserting in Draft Injunction Order

Contempt of Court
Order
Respondent
sent to prison
confidential information relating to Travelgraph

Solicitor
to the Court
set aside this Order
Respondent shall pay the Applicant
Applicant's

DRAFT INJUNCTION ORDER

IN THE HIGH COURT OF JUSTICE   Claim No. 2007 HC 4045

QUEEN'S BENCH DIVISION

MR JUSTICE JACKSON

Date _____

BETWEEN:

_____ (1) Applicant

And

_____ (2) Respondent

_____

DRAFT ORDER FOR AN INJUNCTION

_____

IMPORTANT

NOTICE TO THE RESPONDENT

[1] This Order [prohibits you from doing] [obliges you to do] (3) the acts set out in this Order. You should read it carefully. You are advised to consult a _____ (4) as soon as possible. You have a right to ask the court to vary or _____ (5) .
[2] If you disobey this Order you may be found guilty of _____ (6) and may be _____ (7) or fined or your assets may be seized.

Upon hearing Counsel for the Applicant and Counsel for the Respondent,

IT IS ORDERED that:

THE INJUNCTION

1. For a period of 12 months commencing from 25 February 2007 the _____(8) must not: (i) Enter into or continue in the employment of _____(9); (ii) Divulge to _____(10), their officers, employees and/or agents or to any other person or entity any computer files(s) or _____(11).

COSTS OF THE APPLICATION

2. The _____(12) the costs of this Application.

VARIATION OR SETTING ASIDE OF THIS ORDER

The Respondent may apply _____(13) at any time to vary or set aside this _____(14) but if he wishes to do so he must first inform the _____(15) Solicitors in writing at least 48 hours beforehand.

NAME AND ADDRESS OF APPLICANT'S SOLICITORS

The Applicant's Solicitors are:

Name: _____(16)

Address: _____

Telephone Number: _____

All communications to the Court about this Order should be sent to Room E15 Royal Courts of Justice, Strand, London, WC2A 2LL quoting the case number. The office is open between 10 am and 4.30 pm Monday to Friday. The telephone number is 020 7936 6148 or 6336.

Language practice

Exercise 3 – comprehension

Answer the following questions relating to the above text on injunction orders:

1. What is a 'legal loophole'?
2. What is meant by 'legally watertight'?
3. What does 'jargon' mean?
4. What is meant by 'a layperson'?
5. What is meant by 'being in contempt of court'?
6. What is a 'restrictive covenant'?
7. Under the heading 'Notice to Respondent' in the draft order for an injunction the Respondent is warned that if he does not comply with the terms of the Order then '... your assets may be seized'. What does this mean?

Exercise 4 – modal verbs

In the sentence 'You must not engage in employment with a competitor within a radius of 20 miles for a period of 12 months' the word *must* is a modal verb. Complete the following sentences by inserting an appropriate modal verb in each blank space.

1. The Respondent _____ apply at any time to set aside this order.
2. You _____ not work for a competitor for 12 months.
3. If you do disobey the injunction order your assets _____ be seized.
4. A worker on a building site _____ wear a safety helmet.

Exercise 5 – tense review

Select the correct form of the present tense, past perfect or past simple in each blank space below to complete these sentences.

1. Kadir Salleh _____ (leave) Travelgraph Limited last month.
2. He _____ (join) Travelgraph Limited in 1998.
3. He _____ (work) for Worldlink for a month.
4. After he _____ (receive) the injunction he _____ (consult) a solicitor.

Law notes

Injunctions

- Injunctions are court orders requiring a party to do or refrain from doing something
- A court hearing will be required prior to an injunction being granted
- Injunction applications are almost invariably of an urgent nature
- Injunction applications outside office hours may be considered by a Judge via telephone
- Typical injunction orders include orders preventing:
  1. individuals from contacting another person (such as where the Respondent has previously issued physical threats to or assaulted that other person)
  2. employees from working for a competitor
  3. employees divulging an employer's trade-secrets to a competitor
- Respondent is entitled to three days' notice of injunction application prior to court hearing the application unless secrecy is essential or matter extremely urgent (e.g. applicant is in imminent danger of physical injury)
- An injunction order granted by the court before trial is termed an interim injunction
- A prohibitory injunction prohibits a party from doing something
- A mandatory injunction compels a party to do a specific act

Grammar notes

Modal verbs

Modal verbs can be used to express the speaker's or writer's standpoint, viewpoint or attitude to the matter being referred to in the sentence. (Such as for instance where the matter relates to an instruction, possibility, probability or requirement.) Thus in the injunction order the modal verbs *must* and *may* define what the Respondent must, may or may not do.

Modal verbs are placed before the subject in order to ask a question, otherwise being placed prior to the main verb. Modal verbs have only one form and are followed by the infinitive without 'to'.

Modal verbs include words such as:

must; *can*; *should*; *could*; *may*; *might*; *will*; *would*; *shall*

For instance, to express:

Obligation – *must*; *shall*

Ability – *can*; *should*

Probability – *will*; *may*; *might*

Permission – *may*; *can*

Suggestion – *should*

Request – *would*; *might*

Tense review

Past simple
The past simple is used for actions regarded as completely finished. It is formed by adding 'ed' for regular verbs, as for instance in walk*ed*. We use the past simple when we are talking about completed periods in time. E.g. 'The Judge passed sentence'.

Present perfect
The present perfect is formed by *has / have* + past participle. The present perfect is used to connect the present with the past and is often used with *just; since; ever; yet*.
E.g. 'The Judge has just finished summing up the case'.

Past perfect
This tense is formed by *had* + past participle and is used to refer to an action completed prior to another action in the past. 'Time' words linked with the past perfect include *when; after; before; as soon as*. E.g. 'After the jury had heard the evidence they retired to deliberate on the verdict'.

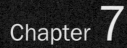

Chapter 7   Breach of contract claim

Learning Objectives

By completing the exercises in this chapter you will:

- Consider modern equivalent language for traditional legal terms
- Practise drafting aimed at ensuring clarity of meaning
- Consider relevant grammar including relative clauses and relative pronouns
- Draft a letter of claim
- Develop word skills specific to drafting Particulars of Claim
- Amend a precedent in order to draft Particulars of Claim

Introduction

The law of contract ('contract law') is an area of *civil law* (as opposed to criminal law). Contract law is concerned with legal rights and remedies resulting from agreements entered into between individuals or companies.

A contract is therefore basically a promise by one party to another which the law recognises as enforceable. A breach of contract arises when one party alleges that another party to an agreement has in some way failed to comply with the *terms* of the agreement. Terms of an agreement may be *express* (i.e. specifically written or stated) or *implied*. Implied terms are mainly created as a result of established *case-law* or *statute*. (For example when a business enters into a contract for the sale of goods the Sale of Goods Act 1979 implies a term into the contract that the goods will be of *satisfactory quality*.)

The party commencing a breach of contract claim is termed the *Claimant*. The party the claim is brought against is the *Defendant*. A breach of contract claim is commenced by issuing proceedings in court (usually the County Court or the High Court for higher value claims). This is sometimes referred to as 'bringing an action'.

The usual *remedy* which the court may order for breach of contract is *damages*. Damages means monetary compensation, usually intended to put the party not at fault in the same position as if the contract had been performed as agreed. (Another remedy the court may grant in certain cases is an injunction, considered in Chapter 6.)

Language practice

Exercise 1 – comprehension

Answer the following questions relating to the above text on contract law.

1. State two *types* of contract you can think of.

2. Is contract law an area of *criminal* or *civil* law?

3. What is meant by the *terms* of a contract?

4. What are the two main types of contract terms?

5. What is meant by *case-law*?

6. What is a *statute*?

7. Is the party bringing a claim the *Claimant* or *Defendant*?

8. What do you consider is meant by the implied term of *satisfactory quality*?

Drafting (i)

Exercise 2 – letter writing

Thomas Shapiro, Managing Director of Travelgraph Limited, is obviously impressed with your abilities, having again come to see you. This time he requires your assistance concerning a matter involving contract law.

In particular, Thomas Shapiro explains to you that Travelgraph Limited purchased two printing machines several months ago at a cost of £45,000 each. Both Travelgraph and the seller signed a written contract on 1 August 2007. The machines were then delivered to Travelgraph's premises on 7 August 2007. These printing machines were purchased for printing the maps and tourist guides which Travelgraph publishes and sells. Thomas Shapiro is very disappointed with these printing machines however since each one is only capable of printing 50 pages per minute. This is half the printing rate that the company which manufactured and sold these machines claimed. (There is an express term in the contract signed on 1 August 2007 stating that each machine would be capable of printing 100 pages per minute.) Travelgraph estimates that it will lose profit in the sum of £200,000 per year from the date of purchasing the machines as a result of this. Thomas therefore wants you to write a letter on behalf of Travelgraph to the company which manufactured and supplied the machines (called 'Matrix Printers Limited'). This is for the purpose of providing notice to Matrix Printers Limited that Travelgraph intends to issue legal proceedings in court for breach of contract unless Matrix Printers offers compensation to Travelgraph for loss of profit.

Complete such a letter to Matrix Printers Limited by filling in the blank spaces in the following letter, using the selection of words and phrases in the panel.

▶

Words and phrases for inserting in letter	
our instructions	contract
breach of contract	express term
legal proceedings	proposals to compensate
satisfactory proposals	act on behalf of

18 BOND STREET
LONDON

TEL. NO : +44 020 7538 2892

SOLICITORS

STRINGWOOD & EVANS

Date: 10 January 2008

Our Reference: T 006

The Directors
Matrix Printers Limited
18 Tottenham Court Road
London
W1 1LB

Dear Sir or Madam:

We _____ [1] Travelgraph Limited of 44 Princess Diana Walk, South Kensington, London, W2 3SL, in relation to a _____ [2] between our client and yourselves. This written contract, entered into on 1 August 2007, stipulated that two 'Ultra-Print 123 Series' printing machines would be supplied by yourselves to our client which would each be capable of printing one hundred A4 pages per minute. It is clear from _____ [3] however that despite this _____ [4] each machine is in fact only capable of printing at a maximum rate of fifty pages per minute. You are therefore liable to our client for _____ [5], as a direct result of which our client has lost anticipated profit to date in the sum of £100,000.

Please provide us with your _____ [6] our client accordingly within fourteen days of receipt of this letter. If no _____ [7] are received within this time then _____ [8] will be commenced without further reference to yourselves.

Yours faithfully,

Stringwood & Evans

Specialist Court and Company Lawyers . . . .

Legal proceedings

Matrix Printers Limited has not replied to the letter you prepared intimating the claim (known as a letter of claim). It is now necessary therefore to commence legal proceedings. In order to do so it is necessary to draft two documents in particular. These are:

A Claim Form

Particulars of Claim

Both of these documents are known as *statements of case*. (Certain other court documents are also statements of case and we will consider those later in this Litigation Section.) 'Statements of case' is a relatively new legal term for these court documents, which were previously known as 'pleadings'. You are likely to find that statements of case often contain a certain amount of old-fashioned language. This old-fashioned style of language has traditionally been used by lawyers when drafting statements of case in order to achieve precision of meaning.

There have however been recent reforms encouraging greater use of plain English by lawyers. In particular, a procedural code known as the 'Civil Procedure Rules' has introduced some new terminology. You should therefore use plain English whenever possible when drafting statements of case, while still ensuring that the meaning of your drafting is precise and unambiguous.

A range of words in legal English sound rather old-fashioned (such as 'ex-parte' and 'pleading'). Some of these words are still used, having proved through time to be particularly apt and descriptive, thereby having become standard or 'stock' phrases. You should however always consider carefully whether there is a plain English alternative.

The following table provides some examples. The first column lists words and phrases which have traditionally been used in statements of case over many years. The second column of the table provides a suitable modern English equivalent for the old-style words and phrases in the first column.

Old-Fashioned Language	Equivalent Modern Language
action	claim
anton piller order	search order
discovery	disclosure
ex parte	without notice (to other parties)
inter-partes hearing	hearing with notice (to other party)
interlocutory hearing	interim (as opposed to final) hearing
interrogatory	request for further information
leave	permission
mandamus order	mandatory order
mareva order (or injunction)	freezing injunction

Continued

prohibition order	prohibiting order
request for further and better particulars	request for further information
setting down for trial	listing (scheduling) for trial
specific discovery	specific disclosure
subpoena	witness summons
summons (to commence proceedings)	claim form
summons for directions	case management conference
thereafter / thereinafter	subsequently / then
therein	contained within

Exercise 3 – vocabulary

In the table below, the first column lists some further examples of old-fashioned language which you are still likely to see today in some legal documentation. The second column provides a selection of suitable alternative modern English words and phrases. Match each expression in the first column with its equivalent in the second column. By way of illustration the first one is done for you.

Old-Fashioned Language	Equivalent Modern Language
aforesaid	in private
aver / plead	in public
in camera	claim form
in open court	stated previously
save that / save insofar	noted below
Plaintiff	claimant
pleading	contend / allege
prescribed by	provided by / indicated by
undernoted	statement of case
writ	except that

▌ Drafting (ii)

Exercise 4

The following document is a claim form. It has been partially completed on behalf of your client. Complete the claim form by entering the correct word (selected from the panel below) in each of the shaded areas of the claim form.

Claimant	claims	contract
Matrix Printers Limited	recover	damages

Claim Form

In the HIGH COURT

for court use only

Claim No.	
Issue date	

Claimant

Travelgraph Limited

Defendant(s)

Matrix Printers Limited

Brief details of claim

The claim is for _____ [1] for breach of a written _____ [2] dated 1st August 2007 made between the _____ [3] and the Defendant for the manufacture and delivery of 2 Ultra-Print 123 Series printing machines. The Claimant also _____ [4] interest pursuant to section 35A of the Supreme Court Act 1981.

Value

The Claimant expects to _____ [5] more than £15,000.

Defendant's name and address

_____ [6]

18 Tottenham Court Road
London
W1 1LB.

	£
Amount claimed	to be assessed
Court fee	
Solicitor's costs	to be assessed
Total amount	

The court office at

is open between 10 am and 4 pm Monday to Friday. When corresponding with the court, please address forms or letters to the Court Manager and quote the claim number.

N1 Claim form (CPR Part 7) (01.02)

Printed on behalf of The Court Service

Exercise 5

The following is a *precedent* for drafting suitable Particulars of Claim for issuing in court on behalf of Travelgraph along with the claim form you have now completed. Lawyers often use precedents to assist with drafting statements of case. A precedent in this sense means a document drafted for a previous and similar type of legal action which is suitable as a 'template' for the document currently required. Always remember however that a precedent will have to be amended to suit the particular circumstances of the case you are working on.

Draft Particulars of Claim suitable for your client's purposes by making appropriate amendments to the precedent below, selecting the correct words or phrases from the alternatives provided in the square brackets. This requires you to delete the words or phrases which are not correct. You will need to take account of the information provided throughout this chapter in order to complete this exercise. By way of illustration the first two in the heading of the Particulars of Claim have been amended for you. (You should assume that today's date is 8 February 2008.)

PARTICULARS OF CLAIM PRECEDENT

IN THE HIGH COURT OF JUSTICE

QUEEN'S BENCH DIVISION   **CLAIM No. 2007 HC 1829**

TRAVELGRAPH LIMITED   **[Claimant]**

AND

MATRIX PRINTERS LIMITED   **[Defendant]**

PARTICULARS OF CLAIM

1. The [Parties / Claimant / Defendant (1)] is and was at all material times a company carrying on business as publishers of maps and tourist guides. The [Claimant / Defendant / Parties (2)] at all material times carried on business as a manufacturer and seller of printing machines.
2. By a [arranged contract/ oral contract / written contract (3)] ('the Contract') entered into between the Claimant and the Defendant and signed by both parties on [17 September 2007 / 18 January 2005 / 1 August 2007 (4)], the Defendant in the course of its business agreed to manufacture and sell to the Claimant and the Claimant agreed to buy from the Defendant 2 Ultra-Print 123 Series printing machines at a price of [£45,000 / £10,000 / £80,000 (5)] each.
3. The Contract included an [implied term / actual term / express term (6)] that the machines would each be capable of printing at a rate of [90 / 100 / 200 (7)] pages per minute using A4 size paper.
4. The Contract included an [applied term / implied term / implicit term (8)] that the machines would be of satisfactory quality.
5. Pursuant to the [action / contract / claim form (9)], on 7 August 2007 the Defendant delivered to the Claimant two printing machines ('the delivered machines') which the [Claimant / Defendant / Respondent (10)] installed at its registered office.

6. [In compliance with / Pursuant to / In breach of (11)] the [omitted / aforesaid / disputed (12)] express and / or implied term, neither of the delivered machines were capable of printing at a rate exceeding [50 / 120 / 100 (13)] pages per minute.

7. As a result of the matters set out above, the Claimant has suffered [loss and damage / interest / compensation (14)].

PARTICULARS OF LOSS

Loss of profit

(a) From 7 August 2007 until 8 February 2008:
(i) estimated receipts from warranted output	£200,000
(ii) actual receipts	£100,000
	£100,000

(b) Continuing from 9 February 2008 at the following annual rate:
(i) estimated receipts from warranted output		£400,000
(ii) estimated actual receipts	[£400,000 / £500,000 / £200,000 (15)]	
		£200,000

8. Further the Claimant claims interest [pursuant to / contrary to / corresponding to (16)] section 35A of the Supreme Court Act 1981 on the amount found to be due to the [Claimant / Respondent / Defendant (17)] at such rate and for such period as the Court thinks fit.

AND the Claimant claims:
(1) [Money / Damages / Satisfaction (18)]
(2) Interest pursuant to section 35A of the Supreme Court Act 1981 to be assessed.

STATEMENT OF TRUTH

The Claimant believes that the facts stated in these Particulars of Claim are true.
Dated this 8th day of February 2008.
Stringwood & Evans, Solicitors, of 18 Bond Street, London.
Solicitors for and on behalf of the Claimant.

Exercise 6 – relative pronouns

Complete the following sentences by inserting the correct pronoun in each blank space from the panel below. (Note that some words may be applicable more than once in this exercise while other pronouns in the panel may not be applicable to any of the blank spaces.)

when	which	that	who	whom

1. The remedy _____ the court may grant for breach of contract is damages.

2. The lawyer wrote a letter to the company _____ manufactured the machines.

3. The individual against _____ a claim is commenced is known as the Defendant.

4. Thomas Shapiro, _____ is the Managing Director of Travelgraph Limited, was disappointed with the printing machines.

▶

Law notes

Contract law

The Particulars of Claim should set out clearly the fundamental details of a breach of contract claim. As illustrated in the example of a Particulars of Claim contained in this chapter, these details should include:

Title of proceedings

Case Number [provided by the court when the proceedings are issued]

Court [here it is the High Court, Queen's Bench Division]

Full Names of each Party to the Proceedings

Status of each Party [i.e. whether Claimant or Defendant]

The contract

Date [1 August 2007]

Parties [Travelgraph Limited and Matrix Printers Limited]

Form [i.e. whether written or oral]

Subject Matter [i.e. what the claim is for]

Consideration [i.e. a promise to confer a benefit on the other party or to incur a detriment. A contract is usually unenforceable in law unless consideration exists. This is to ensure that all parties to the contract are providing something in return for what they are receiving. Here, as is commonly the case, there is consideration in the form of the price being paid]

Terms of the contract [e.g. price agreed etc. Note that terms of the contract which are specifically material to the claim are set out in paragraphs 3 and 4. Note that it is usual drafting practice to set out express terms before implied terms].

Breach of the contract

It is necessary to indicate the term(s) breached, the date(s) and particulars of the breach(es), i.e. what act(s) or omission(s) by the Defendant are being alleged by the Claimant as having amounted to breach of contract. (These details are set out in paragraph 6.)

Loss and damage

It is also necessary to particularise the amount and nature of the loss and damage which it is alleged resulted from breach of contract. (These details are set out here in paragraph 7.) Even if the court determines that there has been breach of contract, the Claimant also has to establish what is termed *causation*. Causation is a legal concept whereby only losses caused as a consequence of the breach are recoverable from the *Defendant*. Such losses are sometimes referred to as having a *causal link* with the breach. Note that in this example past losses are set out first (i.e. losses to date) followed by future losses, the latter being claimed as an annual sum. This is common drafting practice in a case such as this.

Remedies

Here the common remedies for breach of contract are indicated (paragraph 8), i.e. damages and interest.

Statement of truth

All statements of case (including claim forms and Particulars of Claim) must contain a statement of truth in wording similar to that indicated here. This will usually be signed by the party whose statement of case it is (i.e. Travelgraph Limited in this case). Note that where the party is a company, the statement of truth would be signed on behalf of the company by a person holding a senior position within the company (such as a director or company secretary) or by the company's lawyer.

Grammar notes

Relative clauses

Relative clauses provide a mechanism for providing additional information in a sentence concerning a matter, object or person already referred to in the sentence. E.g. in the sentence 'A contract is basically a promise by one party to another which the law recognises as enforceable' the pronoun *which* is used to introduce a relative clause.

There are two types of relative clauses: defining and non-defining. Defining relative clauses are essential to the understanding of a sentence whereas non-defining ones are not. In defining relative clauses commas are not used to separate the relative clause from the rest of the sentence.

> E.g. 'Law is a subject which many people find interesting'. (Defining clause.) 'Tony Blair, who is a trained lawyer, has been Prime Minister since 1997'. (Non-defining clause.)

In relative clauses:

Who is used to refer to people and *which* to things. In defining relative clauses *that* can generally be used in place of any other relative pronoun except *whose*. Note that *whom* is used formally as the object in a sentence.

When the relative pronoun is the subject of a relative clause it cannot be omitted from the sentence, *who*, *which* or *that* being required within the sentence.

> E.g. 'He's the solicitor who drew up the contract.' (*Who* cannot be left out.)

If the relative pronoun is the object of a relative cause it can be omitted.

> E.g. 'He's the solicitor I saw.' (Note that 'whom'/'who' has been omitted.)

Note that if the subject is a person then *which* cannot be used. Conversely, if the subject is a neuter object then *who* cannot be used. *Whose* is used as a relative pronoun instead of using a possessive form. E.g. 'Barristers spend most of their time in court. Their work mainly involves court advocacy.' *Whose* could be used to re-phrase this as 'Barristers whose work mainly involves court advocacy spend most of their time in court.'

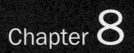

Chapter 8   Road traffic accident!

Learning Objectives

By completing the exercises in this chapter you will:

- Practise using language appropriate to legal correspondence and court proceedings including collocations
- Practise grammar relevant to a civil case including active and passive verb structures
- Analyse the facts of a case
- Enter into legal correspondence on behalf of a client
- Review present and past tenses

A tort claim in negligence

A 'tort' is a breach of a duty imposed by law under what is termed 'the law of tort'. The law of tort imposes a variety of duties on all of us in our daily lives, covering a variety of situations. In this chapter we consider a particularly common tort, the tort of negligence. The purpose of the tort of negligence is to provide compensation for harm suffered as a result of another person's fault. For instance in circumstances whereby someone has caused an accident or made a mistake (such as professional negligence by a doctor or indeed by a lawyer!).

The following criteria must all be met in order to establish that the fault amounts to the tort of negligence (normally referred to simply as 'negligence'):

1. The proposed Defendant owed a duty of care to the Claimant. For instance in the case we look at in this chapter the duty relied upon is one firmly established by case-law, namely that a road user owes a duty of care to other road users.
2. The proposed Defendant breached the duty of care.
3. The damage was caused as a consequence of the Defendant having breached the duty of care. (In other words but for the Defendant's actions the Claimant would not have been injured or suffered loss.) This principle is known as 'causation'.

If the person is acting in the course of his employment at the time of committing the negligent act then the employer is also liable for injury or loss caused as a result of the negligence. This concept is termed 'vicarious liability'.

Exercise 1 – language practice

You have been consulted by a new client named Nicholas Tiessen. Mr Tiessen has been injured in a road traffic accident. You have agreed to act for him in pursuing compensation on his behalf for the injuries he received in the accident. This will involve issuing legal proceedings against the driver responsible for the accident. Firstly however you are required to send the letter on page 74 to your client confirming your instructions.

Read this letter then consider and state whether each of the following statements are true or false based on the contents of the letter. Explain your answer, using the text of the letter to support it.

1. The writer of the letter is declining to act for Nicholas Tiessen.

2. The writer is a solicitor within the banking department of Stringwood & Evans.

3. The firm has a complaints handling procedure.

4. To succeed in his claim it is necessary for Nicholas Tiessen to prove liability beyond all reasonable doubt.

5. There is a good chance that Nicholas Tiessen's claim will be successful.

6. General damages include loss of earnings up to the date of the trial.

Exercise 2

TASK 1

Good letter writing involves being concise. You should therefore think carefully whether a particular word could be used in place of a clause. Enter a word in the second column below which has the same meaning and could be used as an alternative to each of the phrases in the first column. The first entry has been completed for you by way of illustration.

Compound	Simple Form
in the event that	if
at a later date	
as a consequence of	
until such time as	
similar to	
at that particular time	
prior to	
in close proximity to	

TASK 2

Now re-write the following sentence more succinctly.

American courts award damages in personal injury cases which are higher than English courts award when determining damages in the course of making judgements in personal injury cases. ▶

STRINGWOOD & EVANS
18 Bond Street
London
United Kingdom

Tel. No: +44 020 7538 2892

Mr N. Tiessen
27 London Road
Kingston Upon Thames
Surrey
KT4 2LT

30 November 2007

Dear Mr Tiessen,

Accident on 21st September 2007

Further to our meeting yesterday I write to confirm that I will act for you in pursuing a claim against Mr Matthew Gluck and his employer concerning the accident on Friday 21st September 2007. I am a solicitor within the Litigation Department of this firm and will be responsible for the day-to-day work on your file. My secretary, Jennifer Henderson, will be assisting me and can be contacted in the event that I am unavailable at any time you contact this office.

I strive to keep all my clients fully informed and updated concerning the progress of their cases. If you require any clarification of any matter or have any queries at any time however please do not hesitate to contact me.

This firm aims to provide an efficient service and I am confident that we will do so in your case. If however you have any complaints concerning the service being provided that are not resolved to your satisfaction by myself then any such complaint should be addressed to the senior partner, Mrs Christine Stringwood.

If your claim is successful, with liability being established on the balance of probabilities against the Defendants, then you will be entitled to damages. On the basis of the evidence you have provided it is my opinion that your claim has good prospects of success. It may therefore prove possible to negotiate a settlement with the other parties' legal representatives.

There are two main types of damages as follows:-
1. General Damages – in other words compensation for pain, suffering and loss of amenity.
2. Special Damages – meaning actual financial losses incurred up to the date of trial (including for instance loss of earnings etc.).

I will write to you again as soon as there are any further developments with your case.

Yours sincerely,

A. Lawyer

Active and passive verb structures

The active voice

Using the passive verb structure when it is not essential is likely to result in your writing being too formal. This is because it tends to de-personalise the individuals being addressed or referred to. For example:

> *When you arrive you will be met by my secretary. You will be taken to my office, where the conference with counsel will be held.*

Communicating this in the active voice is friendlier and more likely to put your client at ease. For example:

> *My secretary, Jennifer, will meet you when you arrive and take you to my office, where we will be holding the conference with counsel.*

Similarly, the Particulars of Claim in this chapter state that the Ford Galaxy motor car '... *was being driven by the First Defendant*'. This is an example of the passive construction in English and is used as standard practice in court documents and other formal legal documentation. The auxiliary 'be' and the past participle are used. (The passive can be used with any tenses and modal verbs.)

For correspondence purposes however this could be re-written in the active as '... *the First Defendant was driving the car*'. (Here the subject in the passive becomes the object of the active verb.)

Exercise 3 – verb structures

Change the following sentences from a passive to an active construction.

1. The accident was caused by negligent driving.

2. A whiplash injury was diagnosed by a consultant orthopaedic surgeon.

3. The Claimant is being treated by a physiotherapist.

4. The extent of damage to the car will be assessed by a local garage.

Exercise 4 – tense review

Complete the following sentences by entering the correct present or past form of the words in brackets in the blank spaces.

1. I _____ (have) lunch at the moment.

2. Yesterday I _____ (drive) along Regent Street when I had an accident.

3. James _____ (work) full-time at present.

4. At two o'clock this afternoon the aircraft _____ (land) at Luton.

Exercise 5

Legal proceedings have now been issued on behalf of Nicholas Tiessen. The following Particulars of Claim set out details of the claim. Read the Particulars of Claim carefully then complete the following tasks.

IN THE CENTRAL LONDON COUNTY COURT   CASE NO.

    BETWEEN:

NICHOLAS TIESSEN	CLAIMANT
And	
MATTHEW GLUCK	FIRST DEFENDANT
And	
LONDINIUM DELIVERY COMPANY LIMITED	SECOND DEFENDANT

PARTICULARS OF CLAIM

1. At about 4.00 p.m. on Friday 21 September 2007 the Claimant was driving his Honda Accord registration number HL16 GNT along Oxford Street, London, in an easterly direction. At all material times the Second Defendant was the owner of a Ford Galaxy motor car registration number FT23 FLK, which was being driven by the First Defendant as servant or agent for the Second Defendant.
2. A collision occurred when the said Ford motor car, travelling in a northerly direction along Regent Street, drove into the Claimant's vehicle at the junction between Oxford Street and Regent Street. The said junction is a crossroads controlled by traffic lights which were showing green in favour of the Claimant.
3. The collision was caused by the negligence of the First Defendant, acting in the course of his employment.

PARTICULARS OF NEGLIGENCE

The First Defendant was negligent in that he:
   (a) failed to keep any or any adequate lookout;
   (b) failed to observe or heed the presence and progress of the Honda Accord motor car;
   (c) drove too fast;
   (d) drove into collision with the Honda Accord motor car when, by the exercise of reasonable driving skill and care, such collision could have been avoided.
   (e) failed to stop, steer, manage or control his motor vehicle in such a way as to avoid a collision;
   (f) failed to sufficiently apply the brakes of his said vehicle in time or at all. The Second Defendant is negligent by virtue of vicarious liability, being the employer of the First Defendant and owner of the aforesaid Ford Galaxy motor car registration number FT23 FLK.
4. By reason of the matters aforesaid the Claimant has suffered pain and injury, loss and damage.

PARTICULARS OF INJURY

The Claimant, who was born on 18 March 1971, sustained the following injuries:
The Claimant, who was wearing a seatbelt, sustained injury to his neck. Hospital treatment was required, the Claimant having been taken by ambulance to Chelsea and Westminster Hospital, Fulham Road, London. The Claimant was retained in hospital for four days. Following medical examination a whiplash injury was diagnosed. The Claimant was unable to return to work as a computer programmer for five weeks due to continuing symptoms of neck pain, radiating to the right shoulder. This has necessitated physiotherapy treatment, which has now alleviated the symptoms. Full particulars are set out in the medical report of Mr Paulo Jarvis, consultant orthopaedic surgeon, dated 24 November 2007.

PARTICULARS OF SPECIAL DAMAGE

5. (1) Value of Honda Accord motor car damaged beyond repair   £ 7,500
   (2) Loss of earnings: 4 weeks at £1,000 per week   £ 4,000
   (3) Cost of ruined clothing as a result of accident (shirt and jacket)   £ 200
   (4) Cost of 12 sessions of physiotherapy at £25 per session   £ 300

    £12,000

AND THE CLAIMANT CLAIMS:

1. Damages not exceeding £50,000;
2. Interest pursuant to section 69 of the County Courts Act 1984.

STATEMENT OF TRUTH

The Claimant believes that the facts stated in these Particulars of Claim are true.

Nicholas Tiessen

Dated this 2nd day of December 2007.

Stringwood & Evans, Solicitors, 18 Bond Street, London.

Solicitors for the Claimant

Tel. No. +44 020 7126 8983

TASK 1 – COMPREHENSION

Write out answers to the following questions.

1. Name the Defendants.

2. What make of car was your client driving?

3. On what date did the accident occur?

4. Where did the accident occur?

5. Where was Nicholas Tiessen taken immediately after the accident?

▶

6. What is Nicholas Tiessen's occupation?

7. How much income did Nicholas Tiessen lose as a result of the accident?

8. What is the total value of your client's claim for special damages?

9. Why is it contended in the Particulars of Claim that the First Defendant's employer is vicariously liable for the accident?

10. Name one other type of accident you can think of which would conceivably involve negligence.

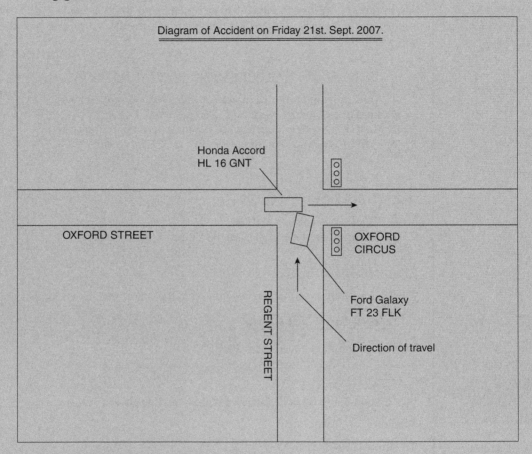

Diagram of Accident on Friday 21st. Sept. 2007.

Honda Accord HL 16 GNT

OXFORD STREET

OXFORD CIRCUS

REGENT STREET

Ford Galaxy FT 23 FLK

Direction of travel

TASK 2 – WRITING

1. Describe the accident in a few sentences, using your own words.

2. Briefly describe your client's injuries, using your own words.

TASK 3 – ACTIVE AND PASSIVE

Imagine that you are about to appear in court. This is to make your submissions to the Judge as to why you contend that the First Defendant was in breach of his duty of care towards your client, the Claimant. Draft your submission in no more than 10 sentences, using the active voice.

Collocations

The English language contains a wide range of vocabulary. When we speak or write in English therefore there are numerous possible word combinations from which to choose. In legal English however it is standard practice to use a number of specific combinations. Becoming familiar with such collocations is an effective way of building your vocabulary.

Exercise 6 – adjective and noun collocations

The first column lists the first parts of some commonly used collocations in legal English which contain an adjective and noun or noun and noun. Complete each collocation by selecting the correct words from the box below. By way of illustration the first entry is made for you.

facts	file	privilege
witness	accident	evidence

car	_accident_
legal	_____
admissible	_____
undisputed	_____
client's	_____
independent	_____
settlement	_____

Exercise 7 – verb and noun collocations

Now complete some commonly used collocations in legal English which contain a verb and noun. By way of illustration the first one is done for you.

out of court	settlement	case	liability
damages	of claim	proposals	statement

take a	_statement_
settle the	_____
award	_____
settle	_____

admit   _____

serve particulars   _____

negotiate   _____

Exercise 8 – letter writing (i)

Complete the following letter to the law firm acting for the Defendants, filling in the blank spaces by selecting relevant phrases from those you have identified in Exercises 6 and 7.

STRINGWOOD & EVANS
18 BOND STREET
LONDON
W1 1KR

▌ + 44 020 7538 2892

Addison, Rais & Partners
18 Aldgate Crescent
London   16 December 2007

Dear Sir or Madam,

N Tiessen v M Gluck and Londinium Delivery Co. Ltd.

We note that you act on behalf of the Defendants in this matter. It appears clear from the facts of the case that the First Defendant caused the _____[1]. We have managed to _____ [2] from an _____ [3] which appears to indicate clearly that liability will be established for negligence.
If the case proceeds to trial we are confident that the court will _____ [4].
To avoid further unnecessary legal costs therefore we look forward to receiving your _____ [5] with a view to seeking to _____ [6] of this case.

Yours sincerely,

Signature

Exercise 9 – letter writing (ii)

Now imagine that you are a lawyer with Addison, Rais and Partners, the firm acting for the Defendants. Write a letter in reply to the one you completed in Exercise 8, denying liability on behalf of the Defendants. Use appropriate phrases from Exercises 6 and 7 in the course of completing the letter.

> Look out for more collocations as you read through this book and come across further legal materials. Also remember to use the glossary and a good dictionary if you are in any doubt (such as *Dictionary of Law*, by L.B. Curzon). The list of collocations at the end of this chapter will also assist you in further developing your legal English vocabulary.

Law notes

The tort of negligence

A *tort* is a breach of a duty imposed by law. The purpose of the tort of *negligence* is to compensate for harm sustained as a result of another's fault. In order to succeed in a legal action for negligence a Claimant must establish:

- A duty of care
- Breach of that duty of care
- Damage resulting from breach of that duty of care (*causation*)

Other torts include:

- *Defamation – libel* if defamatory comments about another are written or broadcast or *slander* if spoken
- *Misrepresentation* – making false or misleading statements which induce someone to enter into a contract
- *Employer's liability* – a duty owed by an employer to employees to provide a safe system of work
- *Vicarious liability* – liability imposed on an employer for torts by employees committed in the course of their employment
- *Breach of various statutory duties* – duties of care imposed by specific Acts of Parliament, including for instance under the Health and Safety at Work Act 1974

Damages in tort
Damages in tort are intended to compensate the Claimant for the loss and/or injury sustained as a result of the tort. In a personal injury case for instance (such as the one considered in this chapter) damages consist of:

- *General damages* – monetary compensation to be assessed by the court, including: compensation for pain and suffering; future medical expenses; continuing loss of earnings etc.;

▶

85

■ Special damages – specific financial loss incurred from date of injury to date of trial, including: loss of earnings up to the date of trial; cost of repair of motor vehicle; medical expenses up to date of trial etc.

Reduction in damages

A Claimant's damages can be reduced by whatever extent the court considers appropriate due to the concepts of:

■ *Contributory Negligence*
Section 1 of the Law Reform (Contributory Negligence) Act 1945 provides that a person's compensation '... shall be reduced to such extent as the court thinks just and equitable having regard to the Claimant's share in the responsibility for the damage'. In other words compensation is reduced to the extent which the court considers the Claimant was personally to blame for his loss. Damages are often reduced for instance in personal injury claims resulting from road traffic accidents (RTAs) if the Claimant was not wearing a seatbelt.

■ *Mitigation*
The law usually requires a Claimant to mitigate his loss. In other words the Claimant must take all reasonable steps to reduce or obviate the loss sustained. For example: John seeks compensation for loss of earnings as a result of being unable to continue in the same employment as previously following a road traffic accident. He will be expected to try to mitigate this loss, such as for instance by re-training or obtaining suitable alternative work.

Grammar notes

Passive structures

In the Particulars of Claim in this chapter it is stated that the Ford Galaxy '...was being driven by the First Defendant'. This is an example of the passive in English and could be re-phrased for spoken English as, 'The First Defendant was driving the car'.

The object of the active verb becomes the subject in the passive.

The passive can be used with any tenses and modal verbs.

Tense review

Present continuous

The present continuous is used to relate events which are currently occurring and is formed by using *am* / *is* / *are* along with the present participle. For example:

'*I am travelling along Regent Street and having an argument with my girlfriend.*'

Past continuous

The past continuous tense is formed by *was* / *were* along with the present participle. It is used to refer to an activity in the past at a particular time. For instance, Jason Garfinkle states in his witness statement (see chapter 9) that he '... *was driving along Oxford Street at approximately 4.00 pm*'.

The past continuous tense can also be used with the past simple tense when an action occurs whilst another event is simultaneously taking place. Thus:

While Jason was driving along Oxford Street he saw an accident.

List of collocations

abandon the claim

abide by the law

accept an offer

accept liability

achieve settlement

address the court

address the meeting

adjourn the case

adjourn the meeting

admissible / inadmissible evidence

admit liability

admit the claim

agree evidence

agree terms

annual general meeting

appeal against the decision

appeal against the judgment

appear before the court

apply the law

argue the case

arrive at a settlement

arrive at the decision

assess damages

attend the meeting

award compensation

award damages

bad accident

board / directors' meeting

break the law

break the rules

call the meeting

call the witness

car accident

case-theory

chair the meeting

challenge the decision

change the law

circumstantial evidence

citizen's arrest

claim compensation

client's file

close the meeting

cogent evidence

coming into force of a statute

comply with the rules

conduct negotiation

conduct the meeting

contradictory evidence

contravene the rules

convene the meeting

corroborate the evidence

counter-argument

County Court

cross-examination

cross-examine the witness

Crown Court

cut-throat competition

declare a dividend

defeat a resolution

defend the case

deliver the verdict

deny liability

deny the claim

direct the jury

discredit the witness

dismiss an appeal

dismiss the claim

draft / re-draft the contract

draft legislation

draw-up minutes

draw-up the contract

enact legislation

enforce the judgment

establish a precedent

examination in chief

examine the witness

exemplary damages

expert witness

extraordinary general meeting

fabricate the evidence

fatal accident

file an appeal

fire / sack / dismiss an employee

float the company

gather evidence

grant an appeal

hand down judgment

hear an appeal

hear the evidence

hearsay evidence

held in custody

High Court

hold the meeting

incriminating evidence

incur costs

independent evidence

independent witness

industrial accident

investigate the case

landmark decision

lead the witness

legal advice

legal authority

legally binding agreement

limited company

lodge the claim

lose an appeal

lose the case

maintain / enforce law and order

make a ruling

manage the company

move towards settlement

multi-national company

negotiate / re-negotiate the contract

negotiate agreement

negotiate settlement

negotiate terms

open the meeting

oppose a resolution

ordinary shares

over-rule the decision

overturn the decision

parent company

pass a resolution

pass legislation

plead the case

preference shares

private company

pronounce judgment

pronounce sentence

propose a resolution

provide an undertaking

provide proof

punitive damages

put forward an offer

put forward proposals

put through legislation

question the witness

reach settlement

recover damages

re-examination

refer to arbitration

register the company

reject an offer

reply to correspondence

reserved judgment

review the case

serve a statement of case

set up a company

settle out of court

settle the case

shareholders' meeting

subsidiary company

summing-up the evidence

sum-up the case

swear in the jury

swear in the witness

take(n) into custody

taking a statement

the court will rise

under arrest

undisputed facts

unsubstantiated allegations

vote against a resolution

vote in favour of a resolution

win an appeal

withdraw an offer

withdraw from the case

withdraw the claim

withhold evidence

Chapter 9 Trial

Learning Objectives

By completing the tasks in this chapter you will:

- Practise vocabulary and grammar required for questioning witnesses
- Understand the concepts of examination in chief and cross-examination
- Amend a witness statement to take account of correct grammar and tenses
- Analyse evidence in a case/prepare a basic case analysis
- Undertake advocacy preparation
- Conduct witness examination using appropriately structured questions and questioning techniques

Advocacy guide

Advocacy is a skill essential to every lawyer, particularly those involved in both civil and criminal court litigation. Effective advocacy requires the ability to present information clearly and to put forward arguments persuasively in order to advance a client's case. Good advocacy involves a combination of language skills, a good range of vocabulary and a sound grasp of grammar. Clear pronunciation is also important. The specific procedure, rules of court and degree of formality expected of an advocate may vary depending on which legal jurisdiction is involved. (For instance courts in the United States of America generally require a less formal approach in terms of dress code and manner of address than English courts.) Nevertheless certain fundamental principles of advocacy are universally applicable.

Examination in chief

An advocate elicits evidence from his or her own witnesses by means of what is termed examination in chief. It is important to remember that the lawyer cannot give evidence. That is the role of the witness, not the advocate. The advocate's job is to get each witness to provide his or her evidence to the court. This is achieved by asking each witness a series of questions intended to develop the client's case.

These questions must be non-leading questions as opposed to leading questions. A leading question is one which suggests the answer, or implies the existence of some particular fact(s) or circumstances and usually prompts a short answer amounting to 'yes' or 'no'. For instance: 'You saw your colleague Henry Hodson steal the money, didn't you Mrs Smith?'

A non-leading question on the other hand does not suggest the answer. Non-leading questions normally start with:

- pronouns such as: 'who'; 'what'; 'where'; 'when'; 'why'; 'how'
- interrogatives such as: 'please explain'

For example: 'What happened next?'

Exercise 1

Read the Particulars of Claim again in the previous chapter concerning Nicholas Tiessen's road traffic accident claim. Then write out four non-leading questions to ask your client Nicholas Tiessen in examination in chief.

Cross-examination

Cross-examination is the stage in a trial when a witness for one party is questioned by the other party's lawyer. A witness is usually cross-examined after having provided his examination in chief. A lawyer is under a duty to put his client's case to the witness when cross-examining. This involves putting his client's version of events to the witness. Well conducted cross-examination can bring further evidence to the court's attention which is of benefit to your client. It can also undermine the other party's case by revealing evidence which questions the witness's credibility or reliability. For instance, by showing that the witness is uncertain about what s/he actually saw, or that s/he is an unreliable witness because of his or her character (e.g. has a criminal conviction), or is biased. Unlike with examination in chief, it is permissible and indeed standard practice to ask leading questions when conducting cross-examination. Leading questions often start with words such as 'did', 'was' and 'were'.

Exercise 2

Now imagine that you are preparing to cross-examine Matthew Gluck, the other driver in the road traffic accident case you considered in the previous chapter. Write out four leading questions to ask him in the course of cross-examination which are aimed at putting your client's case.

(To get you started, an example would be: 'The accident occurred because you weren't paying attention to where you were going, didn't it Mr Gluck?')

▌ Case analysis

Most cases settle before trial. Good litigators nevertheless 'think trial', preparing the case on the premise that it will go to trial. This involves analysing the evidence.

Tasks

TASK 1

Read the following further information which has now become available concerning the car accident case which you considered in the previous chapter.

CASE OF NICHOLAS TIESSEN v MATTHEW GLUCK AND LONDINIUM DELIVERY CO. LTD

FURTHER INFORMATION

1. The defendants have now filed their defence (i.e. the Statement of Case which sets out the defendants' standpoint and response to the claim being made by the Claimant). Liability is denied.
2. Matthew Gluck (the driver of the Ford Galaxy) insists that the traffic lights were in fact showing green in his favour. He is also adamant that Nicholas Tiessen was driving too fast. Also, that Tiessen failed to stop at the junction and failed to obey the traffic lights by driving into the junction when the traffic lights were indicating red against him.
3. Matthew Gluck wears spectacles and has weak eyesight.
4. Matthew Gluck has been convicted of careless driving as a result of the accident.
5. An independent witness has come forward and provided a statement.

TASK 2

Now analyse the case on behalf of the Claimant by identifying two good facts supporting the Claimant's case and two bad facts detrimental to the Claimant's case. State these in the relevant columns below.

Good facts	Bad Facts

TASK 3

The following document is the independent witness statement referred to at point 5 in the Further Information Panel above. It has been drafted by another lawyer in your office who interviewed this witness. Read the witness statement and correct it by putting the verbs in brackets into the correct form in the spaces provided.

WITNESS STATEMENT OF JASON GARFINKLE

1. I [1] .... (be) a forty-seven year old dentist and live at 15 Gray's Inn Road, London. I make this statement concerning a road traffic accident I [2] .... (witness) at the junction between Regent Street and Oxford Street, London, on Friday 21 September 2007. At approximately 4.00 p.m. that day I [3] .... (drive) along Oxford Street towards Oxford Circus. It [4] .... (be) a lovely afternoon and the sun was shining. I [5] .... (come) back from a dental conference at Earl's Court Exhibition Centre and was [6] .... (head) into the West End of town to buy a birthday present for my wife. I [7] .... (drive) behind a blue Honda Accord motor car which [8]........................ (travel) at approximately 30 miles per hour.

2. As I [9] .... (approach) Oxford Circus I [10] .... (can) see that the traffic lights [11] .... (show) green. The aforesaid Honda motor car [12] .... (proceed) through the traffic lights and I [13] .... (begin) to follow. I then suddenly [14] .... (catch) sight of another vehicle off to my right, a silver Ford Galaxy. It [15] .... (head) at high speed along Regent Street towards the Honda in front of me. I [16] .... (can) see that the driver of the silver Ford [17] .... (hold) a mobile telephone. He also [18] .... (appear) to be having an argument with the woman sitting in the front passenger seat of the vehicle. He was clearly not paying attention to his driving or the traffic lights, which were showing red from his direction. The Ford [19] .... (come) straight through the traffic lights into the junction between Oxford Street and Regent Street.

3. The driver of the Ford then [20] .... (brake) hard but his vehicle skidded straight into the driver's door of the blue Honda. I was able to stop just in time to avoid also being involved in the collision. I have no doubt that the driver of the silver Ford was entirely to blame for the accident.

I believe that the facts stated in this witness statement are true.

Signed

Dated

Preparing for trial

The legal profession in England is sometimes described as a 'two-tier profession'. That is because there are two categories of lawyers, namely:

- Solicitors
- Barristers

Most advocacy in English courts is conducted by barristers, who can be thought of as specialist court lawyers. Solicitors can also appear in court. More commonly however a solicitor will fulfil the role of taking instructions from a client and preparing the case. The solicitor will then instruct a barrister to provide the actual representation in court on behalf of the client. These instructions are provided in writing to the barrister in a document prepared by the instructing solicitor called a 'brief to counsel'. This is known as 'briefing counsel', barristers being referred to in court as 'counsel'.

Exercise 3 – brief to counsel

The following is a template for a brief to counsel on behalf of Nicholas Tiessen in the case of *N. Tiessen v M. Gluck and Londinium Delivery Co. Ltd*. Complete this brief to counsel, providing relevant details in under 50 words under each heading.

IN THE CENTRAL LONDON COUNTY COURT   CASE NO. CL4 34756

   BETWEEN:

NICHOLAS TIESSEN   Claimant

And

MATTHEW GLUCK   1st Defendant

And

LONDINIUM DELIVERY COMPANY LIMITED   2nd Defendant

BRIEF TO COUNSEL

Counsel has herewith:

(1) Particulars of Claim and Defence
(2) Statement of Jason Garfinkle dated 10 December 2007
(3) Various correspondence between the parties' solicitors

Instructing solicitors act for the Claimant in this matter. Counsel is instructed to appear on behalf of the Claimant at the forthcoming trial, listed for hearing over two days at Central London County Court on 15 and 16 February 2008. This is a personal injury claim relating to a road traffic accident on 21 September 2007.

ACCIDENT DETAILS

The circumstances of the accident are as follows:

DETAILS OF CLAIMANT'S INJURIES

The details of the Claimant's injuries are as follows:

EVIDENCE

The following details appear to support and strengthen the Claimant's case:

The following details are conceivably detrimental to the Claimant's case:

CONCLUSION

The Claimant has good prospects of success because:

....

Stringwood & Evans

Solicitors for the Claimant

Addressing the court

Advocacy also involves certain inter-personal skills, including non-verbal communication (NVC) or 'body language'. The following is a checklist of principles you should bear in mind in order to become a good and persuasive advocate.

- Enunciate words clearly and speak with sufficient volume
- Address the court at an appropriate pace, ensuring that you do not speak too fast or too slowly
- Modulate the tone and pitch of your voice to maintain the Judge's interest
- Use the correct mode of address to the Judge (i.e. 'Your Honour' or 'Your Lordship' etc.)
- Adopt a suitable posture (for instance do not slouch or put your hands in your pockets)
- Use appropriately formal language (neither pompous nor too colloquial)
- Demonstrate courtesy, a professional manner and ensure a smart appearance (do not make personal comments for instance about the opposing advocate!)
- Avoid distracting mannerisms (such as hand or arm movements)
- Maintain reasonable eye contact with the Judge (while being aware that in some cultures eye contact is regarded as threatening or disrespectful)

Exercise 4 – advocacy preparation

Advocacy practice will develop your advocacy skills, which in turn will increase your confidence in using legal English. Now imagine that you are a barrister who has been instructed to appear in court tomorrow on behalf of the Claimant in a case against a motor car manufacturer. You have received the following brief to counsel from your instructing solicitor. Read this brief to counsel. Then plan and write out several cross-examination questions to put to the defendant's managing director on behalf of the Claimant. (Remember to make these leading questions.)

GOOD PRACTICE TIP: Firstly determine the answers you wish to obtain and then formulate questions which will result in the witness providing the desired answers. Try to keep your questions short.

IN THE KINGSTON UPON THAMES COUNTY COURT	CASE NO. KT4 18932
BETWEEN:	

FERNANDO ESTEBAN	Claimant
And	
HYPERFORMANCE SPORTS-CARS LIMITED	Defendant

BRIEF TO COUNSEL

Counsel is instructed to act on behalf of the Claimant at the forthcoming trial of this action. The basic details of the case are as follows.

The defendant manufactures a range of expensive handbuilt sportscars, including a model known as the 'Mephisto'. The Claimant purchased one of these 'Mephisto' models six months ago, at a cost of £40,000.

The Claimant was injured on 14 August 2007 whilst driving this newly purchased vehicle. The Claimant sustained serious injuries. In particular a broken wrist, fractured collar bone, broken index finger and concussion. The facts of the accident are as follows.

The Claimant was driving his 'Mephisto' car towards Oxford on the M4 motorway at a speed of approximately 70 miles per hour. The car has an automatic gearbox and top gear was engaged. Suddenly the car engaged reverse gear, causing rapid deceleration which resulted in the Claimant's injuries.

The Claimant therefore contends that his injuries were caused as a direct result of the defendant's negligence. Also, that the vehicle was not of satisfactory quality, this being an implied term of the Claimant's purchase contract with the defendant pursuant to section 14(2) of the Sale of Goods Act 1979. Counsel is therefore instructed to argue that the defendant is liable to the Claimant for damages for personal injury and for other financial losses incurred. The latter amount to £10,000, representing the cost of a replacement gearbox (£4,000) and lost earnings of £6,000 (the Claimant being an accountant and having been off work for four weeks).

Instructing solicitors have arranged for a consulting engineer to attend court tomorrow to provide expert evidence confirming that the car suddenly engaged reverse gear. It is the Claimant's case that this clearly establishes negligence on the part of the defendant, since a car should not suddenly go into reverse gear while travelling at 70 miles per hour!

Indeed instructing solicitors believe that the defendant knew about this fault in the gearboxes it fits to the 'Mephisto' models. In particular, there have been several press reports of similar accidents having occurred in England and in the United States, whereby the car has suddenly engaged reverse gear. Counsel is therefore asked to raise this matter with the defendant's managing director in the course of cross-examination.

Counsel should also be aware however that the defendant strongly denies liability, contending that the accident was caused as a direct result of the Claimant's own negligence. The defendant does not dispute that the vehicle went into reverse gear immediately prior to the accident. The defendant alleges however that this was due to the Claimant negligently engaging reverse gear while travelling at speed, thereby inevitably causing the accident. This is vehemently denied by the Claimant. The aforementioned engineer who will be attending court has therefore been asked for his expert opinion regarding this allegation. Unfortunately however the engineer has concluded from examining the gearbox that it is impossible to state with any degree of certainty whether the Claimant changed gear or whether the vehicle 'slipped' into reverse gear due to a mechanical fault in the gearbox.

Counsel is instructed to endeavour to persuade the court to find in favour of the Claimant and to award damages for personal injury and the other losses outlined above.

Delaney & Co.
Solicitors for the Claimant

Exercise 5 – advocacy practice

If you are working with others then undertake the 'Group Exercise' below. Alternatively, if you are working on your own then undertake the 'Individual Exercise' below. Both exercises relate to the case above of *Fernando Esteban* v *Hyperformance Sports-Cars Ltd*.

GROUP EXERCISE

Task 1

Allocate the following roles between yourselves:

■ Counsel (i.e. barrister) for the Claimant
■ Counsel for the defendant
■ The Claimant
■ The Defendant's Managing Director

Task 2

Role-play the trial of *Fernando Esteban* v *Hyperformance Sports-Cars Limited* by adopting the following procedure:

1. Person playing role of Claimant's counsel conducts examination in chief of the Claimant. This should be aimed at setting out the Claimant's case. Claimant answers counsel's questions, improvising with further sensible facts as appropriate in addition to using the details provided in the brief to counsel.

2. Person playing role of Defendant's counsel cross-examines the Claimant, with a view to discrediting the witness and/or his evidence. The cross-examination should also 'put the Defendant's case'. (E.g. that the Claimant caused the accident by carelessly engaging reverse gear himself.)

3. Person playing role of Defendant's counsel then takes the Defendant's managing director through his evidence in chief. Person playing role of the managing director answers counsel's questions based on facts provided in the brief to counsel above and by improvising with further facts and information as appropriate.

4. Counsel for Claimant cross-examines the managing director, seeking to repudiate the witness's evidence and to 'put the Claimant's case' to the witness. (Including for instance that there was a gearbox fault.)

5. Defendant's counsel makes a short 'closing speech', summing up the arguments and evidence in support of the Defendant's case and seeking to dispute the Claimant's claim.

6. Claimant's counsel makes a short 'closing speech', summing up the arguments and evidence in support of the Claimant's case and seeking to contradict the Defendant's version of events.

If there are more people available then you can add further parts to the role-play, i.e. a further person could play the role of the expert witness (the consulting engineer). You should then decide which party will call this further witness for examination in chief, counsel for the other party then conducting cross-examination. A further additional person could play the role of the Judge and decide the case, announcing his or her finding to the court! Everyone present should watch and listen carefully throughout the 'trial', taking note of the evidence presented to the court.

Try to arrange your group as follows for the role-play:

JUDGE

WITNESS (Claimant/Defendant's M.D./Engineer

CLAIMANT'S COUNSEL   DEFENDANT'S COUNSEL

Task 3

Ask one of your colleagues to provide you with feedback on your advocacy performance by completing the following feedback form for you. Alternatively, use this form to provide feedback to one of the advocates on how you assessed his / her advocacy performance.

ADVOCACY FEEDBACK FORM

Provide feedback by grading the advocate's performance under each of the following criteria on a scale of 1 to 5 (1 = unsatisfactory; 2 = poor; 3 = average; 4 = very good; 5 = outstanding).

- Advocate enunciated words clearly ☐
- Advocate spoke at sufficient volume ☐
- Advocate spoke clearly, avoiding long silences and hesitations ☐
- Advocate used language persuasively and expressed herself / himself clearly ☐
- Advocate avoided distracting mannerisms ☐
- Advocate varied his / her tone and pace in order to retain court's interest ☐

ADDITIONAL EXERCISE: Role-play the car crash case of *Nicholas Tiessen* v *Matthew Gluck and Londinium Delivery Company Limited* in a similar manner to the role-play exercise above. This will require you to agree as a group who will play the following roles:

- Counsel for the Claimant
- Counsel for the Defendants
- The Claimant (Nicholas Tiessen)
- The independent witness (Jason Garfinkle)
- The First Defendant (Matthew Gluck)

(Witness and lawyers should use the diagram of the locus (scene) of the accident, p.78, to assist with describing events in this exercise.)

INDIVIDUAL EXERCISE

Task 1

Presume that you are acting as counsel for the Claimant in the case of *Fernando Esteban* v *Hyperformance Sports-Cars Limited*. Plan and write out examination in chief questions aimed at eliciting the Claimant's evidence concerning the following: ▶

- The Claimant's description of the accident
- The Claimant's version of events as to the cause of the accident (the fault in the gearbox)
- The Claimant's response to the allegation that he was at fault for putting the car into reverse gear while driving at high speed
- Details of the Claimant's injuries and other losses

Task 2

Prepare and write out questions to put to the Defendant's managing director in cross-examination in order to put the Claimant's case concerning:

- The alleged cause of the accident (the gearbox 'slipping' into reverse uninitiated)
- The alleged prior knowledge of a fault in the gearbox of the 'Mephisto' model

Task 3

Prepare a short 'closing speech' on behalf of the Claimant, setting out your arguments and referring to the evidence in support of your client's claim.

Task 4

Read out loud the closing speech you prepared in task 3. Ask a friend or colleague to listen to you and then fill in the feedback form at the end of task 3 of the group exercise above for you. Alternatively, self-assess yourself by candidly filling in the feedback form yourself. Keep these criteria and feedback in mind as you further develop and practise your advocacy skills.

ADDITIONAL EXERCISE: Carry out a similar exercise to the one above based on the car crash case of *Nicholas Tiessen* v *Matthew Gluck and Londinium Delivery Company Limited* as follows.

Task 1

Prepare examination in chief questions to ask the Claimant (Nicholas Tiessen) aimed at eliciting the Claimant's evidence concerning:

- The Claimant's description of the accident
- The Claimant's allegations as to why Matthew Gluck was responsible for the accident
- Details of the Claimant's injuries

Task 2

Prepare and write out questions to put to Matthew Gluck under cross-examination in order to put the Claimant's case concerning:

- The allegation that Matthew Gluck drove through a red traffic light
- The allegation that Matthew Gluck was using a mobile telephone
- The allegation that Matthew Gluck was arguing with his passenger

Task 3

Carry out Tasks 3 and 4 in the first individual exercise above.

Law notes

Modes of address

The case you have been considering in this chapter is a County Court case. The correct mode of address to a Judge in the County Court is 'Your Honour'. Here there is no difference in expression between using the vocative case (i.e. addressing the Judge as if by name) and the accusative case (i.e. instead of 'you').

Higher value cases are heard in the High Court, where a Judge should be referred to as 'My Lord / Lady' or 'Your Lordship / Ladyship'. Here there is a difference between the vocative and the accusative case. In particular, 'My Lord / Lady' is the equivalent of the Judge's name (representing the vocative case), whereas 'Your Lordship / Ladyship' is the equivalent of 'you' (i.e. the accusative case). It is however permissible to combine both modes of address in one statement or sentence. For example: 'My Lady, my client has appeared before your ladyship previously.' In addition, when referring to the Judge in the third person the expressions 'His Lordship / Her Ladyship' and 'His Honour / Her Honour' are used. Thus an advocate would say to a witness: 'Please indicate to His Honour using this diagram where you were standing when you witnessed the assault.'

A barrister addresses or refers to a fellow barrister in court as 'My learned friend' and to a solicitor as 'My friend' (vocative case).

Grammar notes

Question forms

Use non-leading questions during examination in chief (unless the facts being referred to are not in dispute). These are usually 'open' questions (i.e. can be responded to with a wide variety of answers e.g. 'What did you see?'). Such questions can begin with pronouns such as 'who', 'what', 'why', 'where', 'when' and 'how' and combined with an auxiliary verb to request information (e.g. 'did', 'has' or 'was'). The question is created by inverting the subject and auxiliary verb. Note however that when the question word is the subject then the auxiliary 'do' should not be used. E.g. 'Who said that?'

Use leading questions for cross-examination. These are generally 'closed' questions (i.e. which limit the scope of possible response, thereby enabling more control over the witness). E.g. 'When did the accident occur?' Aimed at eliciting specific information from a witness, leading questions often start with words such as 'did', 'was' and 'were'. Such auxiliary verbs can be placed before a noun in order to invoke a 'yes' or 'no' response. (E.g. 'Did you see the accident?')

Remember that a question sentence can also be ended with a preposition. (E.g. 'Where was the defendant coming from?') In addition, a question can be conveyed by means of the intonation in one's voice. A rising tone towards the end of a question can thus 'signal' a leading question in particular. (E.g. 'You saw the Ford collide with the Honda, didn't you?')

Chapter 10   Employment law

Learning Objectives

By completing the exercises in this chapter you will:

- Consider language and grammar appropriate to an Employment Tribunal
- Consider reported and direct speech within the context of employment law
- Use appropriate vocabulary in the course of negotiating an employment law case
- Undertake language practice in the course of an unfair dismissal claim
- Acquire an appreciation of the law of unfair dismissal and Employment Tribunal practice and procedure

Unfair dismissal

There is a statutory right in English law not to be unfairly dismissed from employment, as provided by s. 94 Employment Rights Act 1996. An employee normally requires at least one year's service with his or her employer in order to be eligible to pursue an unfair dismissal claim. This qualifying period does not apply however in discrimination cases (such as dismissals based on race, sex, disability, sexual orientation or religious/belief discrimination). There is a three-month limitation period (commencing from the date of dismissal) for issuing a claim for unfair dismissal. The venue for hearing unfair dismissal claims is known as an Employment Tribunal (ET).

The law of unfair dismissal

To defend an unfair dismissal claim an employer must firstly satisfy the Employment Tribunal that the employee was dismissed for a legally acceptable reason pursuant to s. 98 of the Employment Rights Act 1996 (ERA). This includes for instance conduct, capability (including ability or professional qualifications) and redundancy.

A large percentage of unfair dismissal claims are defended on the basis of the employer contending that the dismissal was justified on the first of these grounds, namely conduct. In order for a dismissal on the ground of conduct to be fair in law as opposed to unfair, it must be a reasonable response to the conduct in question.

Alternative possibilities should have been considered by the employer (such as a written warning or demotion as opposed to dismissal).

If the ET determines that the reason for dismissal does not come within s. 98 ERA then it will make a finding of unfair dismissal. If however it is satisfied that dismissal was for one of the legally acceptable reasons it will then consider whether the dismissal was fair in all the circumstances. This involves consideration of whether the employer adopted a fair procedure in the course of dismissal. Including for instance taking into account whether:

- A disciplinary hearing was held prior to dismissal
- The employee was provided with the opportunity to explain his or her version of events
- The employee was provided with a right of appeal

Employment Tribunals have been provided with instrumental guidance on how to approach misconduct cases in the case of *British Home Stores* v *Burchell* 1980 ICR, which held that the ET should consider:

> '... whether the employer ... entertained a reasonable suspicion amounting to a belief in the guilt of the employee of that misconduct at that time.'

This does not mean that the employer must prove guilt but rather:

(a) genuine belief that the employee is guilty of the alleged wrongdoing;

(b) that the employer had reasonable grounds upon which to sustain that belief;

(c) that the employer had carried out as much investigation into the matter as was reasonable in all the circumstances.

An Employment Tribunal is empowered to award damages for losses such as loss of earnings and other benefits (e.g. health insurance) to a Claimant successfully establishing a claim for unfair dismissal.

Exercise 1 – composition

Listed in column 1 below are the first parts of six complete sentences. Complete the sentences by matching each part with its corresponding final part in column 2. The first one is done for you by way of illustration.

Column 1	Column 2
1. Section 94 of the Employment Rights Act 1996 provides	within three months.
2. An employee normally requires one year's service	investigate the circumstances.
3. An unfair dismissal claim must be issued	to be eligible to claim unfair dismissal.
4. An unfair dismissal claim is heard at	state his case when considering dismissal.
5. An employer should permit an employee to	the legal right not to be unfairly dismissed.
6. An employer suspecting misconduct should	an Employment Tribunal.

Employment Tribunal case

You have been consulted by a new client named Charles Edward Scoville. Charles has been dismissed recently by his employer, a firm of solicitors named Bannerman and Law. You have agreed to issue legal proceedings on his behalf for unfair dismissal. Read the following statement of your client, which your secretary has just completed typing for you in readiness for issuing proceedings in the Employment Tribunal. (Assume that today's date is 5 May 2007.)

IN THE EMPLOYMENT TRIBUNAL

BETWEEN:

CHARLES E. SCOVILLE   Applicant

and

BANNERMAN AND LAW (a firm)   Respondent

STATEMENT OF THE APPLICANT

I, Charles Edward Scoville, of 18 Lower Richmond Road, Putney, London, SW15, hereby states as follows.

1. I am the applicant in these Employment Tribunal proceedings. I commenced employment with the Respondent on 16 March 2003. I was based at the firm's Head Office at 11 The Strand, London, WC2, where I worked until 26 April 2007 as one of a team of four legal cashiers.

2. On Monday 26 April 2007 I arrived at the office at approximately 8.50 a.m., to start work as usual at 9.00 a.m. I had just parked in the firm's car-park and was entering the building when I noticed Mr Henry Moore, the firm's Managing Partner, running towards me. He appeared very angry. I was then very taken aback as he grabbed my arm while stating to me 'You're dismissed as of now Scoville. I want your office keys. Don't think you're going anywhere, the police are on their way!'

3. I tried to explain to Mr Moore that I had done nothing wrong and didn't understand what all this was about. I was given no details at this stage of what I was being accused of. All I knew was that I was being summarily dismissed.

4. It was only when the police arrived that I began to get an explanation. Detective Constable Clouseau told me that I was being accused by Mr Moore of stealing several million pounds of client monies. I was astounded by this. I stated in reply that I would never dream of doing such a thing. I have worked as a legal cashier for a number of prestigious legal and accountancy firms in the city and have an unblemished record for my professionalism and honesty.

5. D.C. Clouseau then asked me 'How do you account for the new Ferrari sports-car sitting out there in the car-park then?' I explained that I had been the very fortunate winner of a large sum of money on the National Lottery several days previously. At that time the only purchase I'd made from my winnings was the Ferrari, a vehicle I have longed to own since childhood. Ironically I was intending to continue with my job at Bannerman and Law since I love my work. I also explained this to D.C. Clouseau and his colleague, Police Constable Capriati.

6. The following day I received a letter in the post from Bannerman and Law confirming my dismissal with immediate effect along with a cheque for my salary up to and

including Monday 26 April 2007. The letter was signed by Henry Moore. That day I visited the offices of Chameleon, who run the National Lottery. There I provided Mandy Renwick, Chameleon's Chief Executive, with authority to disclose information to the police confirming my win. When I went to the police station the next day I was relieved to be informed by the police that they had concluded their enquiries and were now satisfied that there were no criminal charges for me to answer. They had received written confirmation from Mandy Renwick that I had indeed recently won the lottery.

7. I have subsequently written a letter to Bannerman and Law asking for an appeal hearing against my dismissal. I want the opportunity to be heard and to explain to the firm that I am entirely blameless. I have not however received any response to my letter to date. I have many friends there and miss their companionship very much. Nevertheless, I no longer want to work for Bannerman and Law after the way I have been treated.

8. The contents of this statement are true to the best of my knowledge and belief.

Signed _Charles E. Scoville_

CHARLES E. SCOVILLE

Date _5th. May 2007_

Exercise 2 – comprehension

Answer the following:

1. State the commencement date and termination date of Charles Scoville's employment with Bannerman and Law.
2. What was Charles Scoville's job title with Bannerman and Law?
3. What reason was Charles given for his dismissal?
4. Is the reason given for dismissal one of the legally acceptable reasons for dismissal? If so, which one?
5. What led the Senior Partner to believe that Charles had stolen from the firm?
6. What explanation has Charles provided for the allegation made against him?
7. What proof has Charles obtained in support of his explanation?
8. State in a few sentences why you would contend that Charles has been unfairly dismissed.

Exercise 3 – drafting

The following document is an application form used for submitting a claim for unfair dismissal to an Employment Tribunal (ET). Boxes 1 to 10 of this application form have been completed on behalf of Charles Scoville. In order to complete the form however it is necessary to set out details of your client's unfair dismissal claim in box 11. Finalise the drafting of this section of the form by selecting the most appropriate form of each verb from the modified verbs in italics. ▶

Application to an Employment Tribunal

- If you fax this form you do not need to send one in the post.
- This form has to be photocopied. Please use CAPITALS and black ink (if possible).
- Where there are tick boxes, please tick the one that applies.

For office use

Received at ET

Case number

Code

Initials

1 Please give the type of complaint you want the tribunal to decide (for example, unfair dismissal, equal pay). A full list is available from the tribunal office. If you have more than one complaint list them all.

Unfair Dismissal

2 Please give your details

Mr ✔   Mrs ☐   Miss ☐   Ms ☐   Other _____

First names   Charles, Edward

Surname   Scoville

Date of birth   19th. January 1968

Address   18 Lower Richmond Road, Putney, London,

Postcode   SW 15

Phone number   020 8798 5322

Daytime phone number   as above

Please give an address to which we should send documents if different from above

Postcode

3 If a representative is acting for you please give details (all correspondence will be sent to your representative)

Name

Address   Stringwood & Evans, 18 Bond Street, London

Postcode   W1 1KR

Phone 020 7538 2892   Fax 020 7538 2894

Reference   SE/CES/001

IT1(E/W)

4 Please give the dates of your employment

From   16th. March 2008   to   26th. April 2007

5 Please give the name and address of the employer, other organisation or person against whom this complaint is being brought

Name   Bannerman and Law

Address   11 The Strand, London

Postcode   WC2

Phone number   020 7458 3462

Please give the place where you worked or applied to work if different from above

Address

Postcode

6 Please say what job you did for the employer (or what job you applied for). If this does not apply, please say what your connection was with the employer

Legal Cashier

7 Please give the number of normal basic hours worked each week

Hours per week

40

8 Please give your earning details

Basic wage or salary

£ 25,000 : 00   per   annum

Average take home pay

£ 1,500 : 00   per   month

Other bonuses or benefits

£   :   per

9 If your complaint is not about dismissal, please give the date when the matter you are complaining about took place

n./a.

10 Unfair dismissal applicants only

Please indicate what you are seeking at this stage, if you win your case

☐ Reinstatement: to carry on working in your old job as before (an order for reinstatement normally includes an award of compensation for loss of earnings).

☐ Re-engagement: to start another job or new contract with your old employer (an order for re-engagement normally includes an award of compensation for loss of earnings).

☑ Compensation only: to get an award of money

11 Please give details of your complaint

If there is not enough space for your answer, please continue on a separate sheet and attach it to this form.

Please see Separate Sheet Attached.

12 Please sign and date this form, then send it to the appropriate address on the back cover of this booklet, (see postcode list on pages 15-17).

Signed

Date

IT1(E/W)

CHARLES E. SCOVILLE v BANNERMAN AND LAW

SECTION 11

1. I *to begin / beginning / began* [1] employment with Law and Bannerman ('the Respondent') on 16 March 2003. I *employing / was employed / to employ* [2] as a legal cashier, *worked / to work / working* [3] in a team of four within the Respondent's accounts department. My work principally involved double-entry book-keeping of the firm's client account and client ledgers. The Respondent is an international law firm, *have / having / to have* [4] several overseas offices.

2. At my annual appraisal meeting in March 2007 I was *telling / to tell / told* [5] by my manager that management were very pleased with my work. I was *to give / given / give* [6] a pay rise to reflect this. I have never received any disciplinary warnings.

3. However on Monday 26 April 2007 I *arriving / to arrive / arrived* [7] at work as usual at about 8.50 a.m. I am in the habit of *driving / drove / to drive* [8] to work since there is a staff car-park. I had just parked and was *to enter / entering / enter* [9] the building when I was suddenly confronted by Mr Henry Moore, the Respondent's Managing Partner. He started *shouting / shout / to shout* [10] at me. I was shocked and confused. Then he suddenly *to tell / told / tell* [11] me I was sacked. I tried to reason with him but he was too angry to listen.

4. Shortly after that the police *arrived / arrive / to arrive* [12]. They *inform / to inform / informed* [13] me that I was being accused of stealing a large amount of money from the Respondent. I told Detective Constable Clouseau that was absurd. I *to explaining / explained / explain* [14] that I had done nothing wrong. The police subsequently accepted this and discontinued their enquiries.

5. I was nevertheless summarily *dismiss / to dismiss / dismissed* [15] on Monday 26 April 2007 for alleged gross misconduct. I therefore respectfully *contend / contending / to contend* [16] that I have been unfairly dismissed. There was no valid nor acceptable reason for my dismissal.

6. My dismissal was also procedurally unfair. In particular I was not granted a disciplinary hearing. I was therefore *to deny / deny / denied* [17] the opportunity *providing / to provide / provide* [18] an explanation. In addition I have been denied an appeal hearing.

■ Notice of appearance

The Employment Tribunal (ET) imposes a time-limit of three weeks on an employer in which to respond to an employee's claim for unfair dismissal. The correct form for providing this response is known as a 'Notice of Appearance'.

Exercise 4 – drafting

Now assume that you are a lawyer in the Employment Law Department of a law firm called Weir and Company. Weir and Company has been consulted by Bannerman and Law, who intend to resist the unfair dismissal claim issued against them by Charles Scoville. Read the following statement by Henry Moore, the Managing Partner who dismissed Charles Scoville. Then complete the following Notice of Appearance form on behalf of Bannerman and Law by setting out in box 7 of this form the Respondent's case. You should take into account the details provided in the Managing Partner's statement when completing these details. (Finally check your answer with the suggested draft in the Answer Key).

IN THE EMPLOYMENT TRIBUNAL   CASE NO.

BETWEEN

CHARLES E. SCOVILLE   Applicant

and

BANNERMAN AND LAW (a firm)   Respondent

<u>WITNESS STATEMENT OF HENRY J. MOORE</u>

I, Henry Jason Moore, of 48 The Meadows, Westminster Village, London, hereby states as follows,

1. I am Managing Partner of the Respondent. The Respondent is a commercial law firm with forty partners and approximately two hundred associate solicitors. We have regional offices in Piraeus, Kuala Lumpur, Moscow and Monte Carlo. We act mainly for clients with shipping and aviation acquisition, financing and litigation work.

2. On Monday 26th April at approximately 8.30 a.m. I was in a meeting with the Chief Executive of Image International, the advertising agency the firm uses. This was taking place in my office at Bannerman and Law's Head Office premises at 11 The Strand, London. Suddenly we were interrupted by Joan Winter, my personal secretary. Joan informed me that Geoffrey Hamilton, our Chief Accountant, needed to speak to me very urgently. I therefore took Geoffrey's telephone call straight away. He sounded very upset and it soon became clear why. The Finance Department had just discovered that an unauthorised withdrawal of two million pounds had been made from the firm's client account at some time during the weekend. Geoffrey and his department were desperately trying to ascertain where the money had gone.

3. I immediately concluded my meeting with Gordon Manderson, Image International's Chief Executive. I was very concerned about what Geoffrey Hamilton had told me. I knew the situation was a very serious matter as far as the firm was concerned. Our professional body, The Law Society, had to be informed in accordance with our rules of conduct. Indeed I spent nearly an hour on the telephone that morning speaking to Janet Adamson, the Senior Officer in the Professional Ethics Department at the Law Society. She was only persuaded not to send a full team of investigators into our office that day as a result of me providing a personal

109

undertaking. An undertaking that I and my fellow partners would restore the missing funds in client account from our personal resources by close of business that day.

4. I then convened a video conference between the partners in London and the overseas offices. We agreed at that time that it was crucial to find out who had misappropriated the funds in order to assure clients of the continued integrity of the firm. During the video conference I switched on the television in the conference room and was horrified to see a report on the local news programme about Bannerman and Law, solicitors and the missing £2 million.

5. As I was moving back from the television to the conference table I glanced out of the window. That was when I saw Charles Scoville, one of our cashiers, pull up in the carpark driving a new Ferrari 355. I knew at that moment we had found the culprit. It was obvious for anyone to see. Charles joined Bannerman and Law several years ago and there's no way his salary would have enabled him to drive such a vehicle.

6. So I excused myself from the meeting and ran downstairs to reception. Charles was just coming into the building when I got down there. I went straight up to him and confronted him. I shouted at him that he was dismissed with immediate effect and that I wanted his office keys. He looked very taken aback and pale as he handed me his office keys. He was clearly upset but said nothing in reply, convincing me further he was the thief of the £2 million.

7. Pauline, our receptionist, also looked surprised at what was going on. I told her to telephone the police and to ask them to send an officer round straightaway to arrest the man we now knew to be the thief of the £2 million. I then waited with Charles Scoville to make sure he didn't escape. Charles kept asking what this was all about but I refused to enter into a discussion with him. I simply replied, 'You know what this is all about.'

8. Detective Constable Jack Clouseau arrived shortly afterwards along with Police Constable Anne Capriati. I was surprised that they did not immediately arrest Charles. Instead they explained to him he was not under arrest and asked him if he would nevertheless voluntarily answer a few questions. Charles said he was happy to do so and that he just wanted someone to explain to him what was going on.

9. I told D.C. Clouseau not to be fooled by him, but he and his colleague then went into a nearby interview room with Charles Scoville. After telling a few clients who'd been passing through reception what had happened I then went up to the Human Resources Department. There I instructed the Head of Personnel to send a letter out in the post to Charles Scoville that day confirming his dismissal and enclosing a cheque for his salary up to that day. The letter also stated that the firm would be taking legal proceedings against him for return of the money. I then went back upstairs and congratulated myself on finding the culprit by pouring myself a glass of wine from the drinks cabinet in the conference room.

10. The contents of the statement are true to the best of my knowledge and belief.

Signed   *Henry J. Moore*

        HENRY J. MOORE

Date   *19th. May 2007*

EMPLOYMENT TRIBUNALS

In the application of CHARLES E. SCOVILLE -v- BANNERMAN & LAW

Case Number
(please quote in all correspondence)

* This form has to be photocopied, if possible please use Black Ink and Capital letters .
* If there is not enough space for your answer, please continue on a separate sheet and attach it to this form

1. Full name and address of the Respondent:

Bannerman & Law,

11 The Strand,

London

Post Code: WC2

Telephone number:

020 7458 3462

2. If you require documents and notices to be sent to a representative or any other address in the United Kingdom please give details:

Weir & Co.,

Solicitors,

45 Richmond Hill,

Richmond,

Surrey

Post Code: KT8 9BU

Reference: A/B&L/01

Telephone number: 020 8431 8907

3. Do you intend to resist the application? (Tick appropriate box)

YES ✓   NO ☐

4. Was the applicant dismissed? (Tick appropriate box)

YES ✓   NO ☐

Please give reason below

Reason for dismissal:
GROSS MISCONDUCT

5. Are the dates of employment given by the applicant correct? (Tick appropriate box)

YES ✓   NO ☐

please give correct dates below

Began on

Ended on

6. Are the details given by the applicant about wages/salary, take home or other bonuses correct? (Tick appropriate box)

YES ✓   NO ☐

Please give correct details below

Basic Wages/Salary	£	per
Average Take Home Pay	£	per
Other Bonuses/Benefits	£	per

PLEASE TURN OVER

For office use only
Date of receipt   Initials

Form IT3 E&W - 8/98

7. Give particulars of the grounds on which you intend to resist the application.

8. Please sign and date the form.

Signed   Dated

DATA PROTECTION ACT 1984
We may put some of the information you give on this form on to a computer. This helps us to monitor progress and produce statistics. We may also give information to:
* the other party in the case
* other parts of the DTI and organisations such as ACAS (Advisory Conciliation and Arbitration Service), the Equal Opportunities Commission or the Commission for Racial Equality.
Please post or fax this form to : The Regional Secretary

* IF YOU FAX THE FORM, DO NOT POST A COPY AS WELL
* IF YOU POST THE FORM, TAKE A COPY FOR YOUR RECORDS

Form IT3 E&W 8/98

Exercise 5 – language practice (i)

The following phrasal verbs are commonly used in legal English:

sue for damages	call for the witness	take down a statement	draw up a court order

Complete the following sentences by inserting the appropriate phrasal verb from those above into each of the blank spaces below.

1. We expect the Judge to _____ shortly.

2. My lawyer has told me he is now going to _____ for approval by the court.

3. I have arranged for my secretary to _____ from the independent witness.

4. If you do not compensate my client for your negligence he will _____ .

Exercise 6 – language practice (ii)

Complete the following statements by selecting the correct expression to place in the blank spaces from the list of single-word adverbs and multi-word adverbial expressions in the panel below.

1. I _____ _____ you accept the present offer.

2. Our offer is an _____ _____ one.

3. I do _____ _____ that the contents of my statement are true.

4. The Defendant _____ _____ the claim against her.

5. The negotiation was _____ _____ .

6. You will need to _____ _____ your present offer if settlement is to be achieved.

7. The Claimant was _____ _____ in the course of his work.

8. A Judge must be _____ _____ in the course of arriving at his decision.

9. An advocate must never _____ _____ the court.

10. The court ordered the Defendant to _____ _____ working for a competitor.

11. The employee was _____ _____ _____ .

12. My client is hoping to _____ _____ _____ _____ .

extremely generous	severely injured	deliberately mislead
solemnly declare	strongly suggest	successfully defended
dismissed without notice	totally objective	settle out of court
substantially increase	refrain from	extremely fruitful

Negotiation

The majority of cases (including Employment Tribunal cases) are settled prior to a full hearing. This means that the parties in the case have negotiated terms of settlement, thereby preventing the need for a court or tribunal hearing. This is sometimes referred to as 'settling out of court'. Negotiation can be conducted by correspondence, telephone or by electronic communication such as e-mail as well as by means of a personal meeting between the parties and their lawyers. In order to negotiate effectively it is important to ascertain:

- The details of your client's case
- The relevant law
- Your client's aims and goals
- The strengths, weaknesses and value of your client's case

Exercise 7 – letter writing

Following further advice from Stringwood & Evans, Charles Scoville has now confirmed that he would accept the sum of £25,000 in settlement of his claim. The following letter is addressed to Roderick Krugman, the lawyer acting for Bannerman and Law and sets out without prejudice proposals for settlement in accordance with Charles Scoville's instructions. ('Without prejudice' means that the correspondence will remain confidential between the parties in the event that no settlement is reached.) Complete this letter by inserting the correct words from the box below into the corresponding spaces in the letter.

prospects of success	damages	award
Employment Tribunal	unfairly dismissed	mitigate
settlement	applicant	instructions
misconduct	disciplinary hearing	dismissal

STRINGWOOD & EVANS
18 BOND STREET
LONDON
W1 1KR

▌ +44 020 7538 2892

30 May 2007
Weir & Co.,
45 Richmond Hill,
Richmond,
Surrey,
KT8 9BU.   WITHOUT PREJUDICE

Dear Mr Krugman,

Charles E. Scoville v Bannerman and Law

We act on behalf of the [1] _____ in the above [2] _____ _____ proceedings.
It appears clear from our [3] _____ that our client has been [4] _____ _____ .

In particular, there does not appear to have been any valid nor acceptable reason for his
[5] _____ . The dismissal was also procedurally unfair. For instance Mr Scoville was
not provided with the opportunity to explain, there having been no [6] _____
_____ . Similarly, he was denied his legal right to have a representative present
when confronted with the allegation of [7] _____ . We are confident therefore that
our client's [8] _____ _____ _____ are high.

Mr Scoville has not obtained further employment despite having made efforts to
[9] _____ his loss. We are confident therefore that the Employment Tribunal would
[10] _____ significant [11] _____ .

Entirely without prejudice however, we would propose [12] _____ of this matter on
the basis that your client pays the sum of £25,000 within 21 days.

Yours sincerely,

Exercise 8 – vocabulary

There are different styles of negotiation. For instance you may take a co-operative, conciliatory or competitive approach when negotiating. Adopting the latter approach involves making more use of 'aggressive' vocabulary, whereas adopting a co-operative or conciliatory approach involves more use of 'diplomatic' vocabulary. Note for instance the following expressions:

(a) Your offer is ridiculous.
(b) I wonder if you could reconsider your offer.

(a) is an example of aggressive vocabulary, whereas (b) is an example of diplomatic vocabulary.

Now indicate which phrase in each of the following pairs is the diplomatic form of expression and which one is the aggressive form (writing the initial 'D' alongside the diplomatic form and 'A' alongside the aggressive form).

(c) If settlement is not reached very soon we will proceed to a tribunal hearing.
(d) We would prefer to reach an early settlement in order to avoid a tribunal hearing.

(e) We demand that our client is provided with a reference.
(f) We are instructed to request a reference.

The Employment Tribunal

Employment Tribunals have jurisdiction over most employment law related cases including unfair dismissal and discrimination in employment cases (including sex, race and disability discrimination). Employment Tribunals usually consist of three 'panel members', consisting of a chairperson (who must be legally qualified as a solicitor or a barrister) and two 'lay' members who are not lawyers. The Tribunal's decision is reached by a unanimous or majority decision. In other words if there is disagreement between the panel members then the majority decision prevails.

The procedure for hearing tribunal cases is similar to usual court procedure (as described in the previous chapter). Employment Tribunal proceedings are however more informal. For instance an Applicant or Respondent is entitled to act for themselves or appoint someone to represent them who is not legally qualified. Thus anyone has 'rights of audience' in an Employment Tribunal.

Exercise 9 – preparing for the Employment Tribunal

Bannerman and Law have rejected the settlement offer put forward by Stringwood & Evans on behalf of Charles Scoville. It is now necessary therefore to prepare for the Employment Tribunal hearing.

1. Read carefully the following witness statements from Detective Constable Jack Clouseau and Mandy Pauline Renwick.

2. Then complete the following case-plan on behalf of Charles Scoville in readiness for the hearing, taking account of all the information now provided to you on the case.

IN THE EMPLOYMENT TRIBUNAL   CASE NO. 128942/02

BETWEEN

CHARLES E. SCOVILLE   Applicant

and

BANNERMAN AND LAW (a firm)   Respondent

I, Detective Constable Jack Clouseau, care of Bow Street Police Station, Ludgate Hill, London, hereby states as follows

1. On the morning of Monday 26 April 2007 I was on duty at Bow Street Police Station. Acting on information received I attended the office of Bannerman and Law, solicitors, at 11 The Strand, London at 9.45 a.m. that morning along with P.C. Capriati.

2. As we arrived a middle-aged man came to the main entrance to meet us, identifying himself as Mr Henry Moore, Managing Partner of Bannerman and Law. He appeared quite agitated, intimating 'I've got him, the multi-million pound, Ferrari driving swindler!'

3. Mr Moore was insisting vehemently that we should arrest another individual also in the reception area who he kept pointing to. Mr Moore was remonstrating that this other individual, who he referred to as Charles Scoville, had stolen £2 million from Bannerman and Law. Mr Moore clearly wanted us to arrest this man and take him into custody.

4. P.C. Capriati tried to calm Mr Moore down while I spoke to the other man, who confirmed he was indeed Charles Scoville. Mr Scoville also told me that he was employed as a cashier with Bannerman and Law, had done nothing wrong and had no idea what Henry Moore was going on about.

5. P.C. Capriati and I then invited Mr Scoville to come with us into a small empty office adjoining the reception area. We explained to Mr Scoville that he was not under arrest and that we merely wanted to have an informal chat with him. This was with a view to establishing the full situation. Charles Scoville replied 'Please, call me Charles. I am more than happy to co-operate. I am an entirely innocent party in all this!'

6. My colleague and I therefore went into the small office with Charles Scoville and explained to him that Mr Moore was alleging he'd misappropriated £2 million from Bannerman and Law. Charles Scoville replied 'That's ridiculous, why on earth should he think that? Oh good grief wait a minute! It's the Ferrari isn't it?' He then went on to explain that on the Wednesday of the previous week he'd been one of three lucky jackpot winners of the national lottery and had won just over £4.8 million. He hadn't told anyone apart from immediate family. I asked Charles Scoville for his full name, address and date of birth, which he provided. I then arranged for him to attend Bow Street Police Station two days later. By then I hoped to have had the opportunity of investigating matters further.

7. At 9 a.m. on Wednesday 28 April 2007 I attended the registered office of Chameleon Gaming Systems at 148 The Mall, London, operators of the National Lottery. There I

spoke to Mrs Mandy Renwick, Chief Executive of Chameleon. She confirmed to me that Charles Scoville had indeed been a lottery winner the previous week, winning £4.8 million.

8. Further investigation then revealed that the missing £2 million was in fact paid back into the client account of Bannerman and Law on Tuesday 27 April 2007. Also, that it had actually been withdrawn by another partner at the firm, who had been trading the money speculatively on the international money market at weekends. On previous occasions these monies had been paid back into the firm's client account prior to the start of the working week. However a delay in the transfer of the funds on the night of Sunday 25 April due to a delay in the opening of the Tokyo stock exchange had triggered this whole situation. When Charles Scoville attended Bow Street Police Station at 4.00 p.m. on Wednesday 28 April I therefore informed him accordingly that no further police action was being taken in this matter.

9. The contents of this statement are true to the best of my knowledge and belief.

Signed _____

        D.C. Clouseau

Date _____

IN THE EMPLOYMENT TRIBUNAL   CASE NO. 128942/02

BETWEEN

CHARLES E. SCOVILLE   Applicant

And

BANNERMAN AND LAW (a firm)   Respondent

I, Mandy Pauline Renwick, care of 148 The Mall, London, hereby state as follows.

1 I am Chief Executive of Chameleon Gaming Systems P.L.C., hereinafter referred to as 'Chameleon'. Chameleon possesses the Governmental licence to operate the National Lottery throughout the United Kingdom.

2 As requested by Mr Charles Edward Scoville I can confirm that he was one of three 'Jackpot' winners of the National Lottery draw on Wednesday 21 April 2007. Mr Scoville's winnings amounted to £4.8 million, paid to an account in his name at Global Security Bank, 44 Piccadilly, London by telegraphic transfer on Friday 23 April 2007.

3 The contents of this statement are true to the best of my knowledge and belief.

Signed _____

        M.P. RENWICK

Date _____

CASE-PLAN

A. THE CLIENT'S AIMS / GOALS.
Set out below the client's main aims / goals.

B. ARGUMENTS IN FAVOUR OF YOUR CLIENT'S CASE AND SUPPORTING EVIDENCE.
Indicate below two arguments in favour of your client's case. Also identify any specific sources of evidence in support of these arguments.

C. ARGUMENTS YOU ANTICIPATE WILL BE MADE BY THE OTHER PARTY.
Provide two examples of arguments you anticipate will be made by the Respondent's representative. Also indicate briefly how you will counteract these in the course of negotiation.

Exercise 10 – Employment Tribunal hearing

If you are working on your own then undertake the 'Individual Exercise' below. Alternatively, if you are working in a group then undertake the 'Group Exercise' below. Both exercises relate to the above case of *Charles E. Scoville* v *Bannerman and Law*.

INDIVIDUAL EXERCISE

Imagine that you are the chairperson of the Employment Tribunal hearing Charles Scoville's case and carry out the following tasks.

1. Consider carefully all the evidence and details of the case, taking notes of information you consider to be relevant to the case as you read through:

   ■ Charles Scoville's Application;
   ■ the Notice of Appearance;
   ■ the witness statements.

▶

2. Write a Tribunal decision of approximately one page in length, referring to the evidence and details available.

GROUP EXERCISE

Task 1

Allocate the following roles between yourselves:

■ the Applicant (Charles Scoville)
■ the Applicant's Representative
■ the Respondent's Managing Partner (Henry Moore)
■ the Respondent's Representative

Task 2

Role-play the Employment Tribunal hearing of the *Charles E. Scoville* v *Bannerman and Law* case by following the under-noted procedure:

(a) Person playing role of Respondent's Representative conducts examination in chief of the Respondent's Managing Partner (Henry Moore). Endeavour to set out the Respondent's case. Person playing role of Henry Moore answers the Representative's questions, improvising with further sensible details as appropriate in addition to using the details provided in the Applicant's Application, the Notice of Appearance and the witness statements.

(b) Person playing the role of Charles Scoville's Representative cross-examines Henry Moore, with a view to contradicting his evidence and putting the Applicant's case.

(c) Person playing the role of Charles Scoville's Representative then calls Charles Scoville (the Applicant) to give his evidence, taking the Applicant through his examination in chief. Person playing the role of the Applicant answers the Representative's questions based on the details provided in the Applicant's Application, the Notice of Appearance and the witness statements as well as by using further improvised facts and information as appropriate.

(d) Person playing the role of the Respondent's Representative then cross-examines the Applicant, seeking to repudiate the Applicant's evidence and to put the Respondent's case to the witness.

(e) The Applicant's Representative makes a short closing speech, summing up the arguments and evidence in support of the Applicant's case and seeking to dispute the Respondent's arguments and version of events.

(f) The Respondent's Representative makes a short closing speech, summing up the arguments and evidence in support of the Respondent's case and seeking to contradict the Applicant's case.

If there are more people within your group then you should add further roles to the role-play. For instance a further person could play the role of Mandy Renwick. (The Applicant's Representative could call this further witness for examination in chief, the Representative for the Respondent then conducting cross-examination. A further person could play the role of Detective Constable Clouseau in a similar fashion.)

If there are remaining members of your group then appoint three of them as panel members of the Tribunal. These three should then consider and announce a decision after hearing all the evidence. Everyone present should watch and listen carefully throughout the hearing, taking notes of the evidence.

Try to arrange your group as follows for the role-play.

EMPLOYMENT TRIBUNAL PANEL

WITNESS (Applicant / Henry Moore / D.C. Clouseau / Mandy Renwick)

RESPONDENT'S REPRESENTATIVE   APPLICANT'S REPRESENTATIVE

Exercise 11 – reading and pronunciation

Charles Scoville's case has now been heard and the Employment Tribunal has issued a written decision (pp. 117–19).

1. Read out loud the following words from the judgment, taking care to use correct stress patterns.

2. Write the correct stress pattern above each word in the panel. By way of example, the first one is done for you, showing the correct stress pattern above the word 'decision'. (The phonetic /s/ being found in 'si' in this word.)

decision (de-ci-sion)	dismissal	conduct	considered
procedure	fairness	information	hearing
representative	misconduct	investigation	evidence
allegation	admission	employer	wrongdoing
misappropriation	tribunal	declare	Respondent

3. Read out the decision, paying attention to your pronunciation.

   (If you are working with others then work in pairs, taking turns to read out the decision to each other. Provide feedback to your partner on his or her pronunciation, identifying any specific words which you consider are being incorrectly pronounced.)

▶

THE EMPLOYMENT TRIBUNAL

CASE NO. 128942/02

BETWEEN

Applicant   Respondent

Charles E. Scoville   AND   Bannerman and Law (a firm)

DECISION OF THE EMPLOYMENT TRIBUNAL

HELD AT: London (Central)   ON: 27 AUGUST 2007

CHAIRMAN: Mr Claude Rumbelow   MEMBERS: Thomas Stringfellow

                                                                                Carol Kendall

Appearances

For Applicant: Richard Vaughan,   Counsel and

                        Nancy Watkins,   Solicitor

For Respondent: Jonathan Stevenson,   Counsel and

                           Samantha Ponsonby,   Solicitor

DECISION

The unanimous decision of the Tribunal is that: the Applicant was unfairly dismissed.

THE DECISION OF THE EMPLOYMENT TRIBUNAL

The tribunal has reached a unanimous decision in this matter. Firstly it is accepted that there was a dismissal. What was however in dispute was whether the dismissal was fair or unfair. The Respondent contended the former and the Applicant the latter.

The Respondent is a city firm of solicitors, being a partnership with its head office in London. It also has four overseas offices. The Applicant was employed as a legal cashier for approximately 4 years prior to being dismissed by the Respondent on 26 April 2007. The Respondent contends the dismissal was justified by reason of gross misconduct.

We are satisfied that the reason for dismissal was the employee's conduct relating to the alleged theft of £2 million. This is a potentially fair reason for dismissal as provided by section 98 of the Employment Rights Act 1996 (ERA). We then considered whether the dismissal was fair in all the circumstances, as further required by section 98(4) ERA.

A relevant issue here was whether the employer had adopted a fair procedure in the course of dismissal. The Advisory, Conciliation and Arbitration Service (ACAS) Code of Practice on Disciplinary Procedure provides a helpful set of guidelines. It states that the following matters should be taken into account by an employer in the course of taking disciplinary action against an employee in order to ensure procedural fairness. The employee should be provided with detailed information concerning the allegations in advance of the disciplinary hearing (preferably in writing). The employee should also have the opportunity to make representations in his or her own defence. The employee is also entitled to be accompanied by a representative at a properly convened disciplinary hearing.

We also took into account the instrumental finding in *British Home Stores* v *Burchell* 1980, as recently confirmed by *Boys and Girls Society* v *MacDonald*. This was in relation to considering the reasonableness of the employer's actions in dismissing the employee in the particular circumstances.

These cases held that in order for the dismissal to be fair in a case of alleged misconduct the employer must satisfy three criteria. Firstly that the employer genuinely believed the employee had done wrong. Secondly that there were reasonable grounds for that belief. Thirdly that the employer reached that conclusion of misconduct after having carried out a reasonable investigation into the matter.

In the tribunal's view it was clear from the evidence we heard that this dismissal was procedurally unfair. Virtually none of the above requirements for a fair dismissal were adhered to by the employer. The Applicant was 'ambushed' by Mr Moore, the Respondent's Managing Partner. In other words the Applicant was dismissed without being provided with any advance notice of the allegation being made against him. Nor was he provided with the opportunity to reply to the allegation. Similarly, details of the allegation were not even made clear to the Applicant at the time of dismissal. Neither was there any proper disciplinary hearing. Quite simply Mr Moore had already made up his mind that the Applicant had stolen this money without even listening to what he had to say in response.

By Mr Moore's own admission he summarily dismissed the Applicant in front of colleagues. He also divulged details of Mr Scoville's dismissal to a number of clients in reception. It further appears from the evidence that there was no reasonable or proper investigation carried out. Mr Moore simply leapt to the conclusion that the Applicant was the culprit. This procedural unfairness was then compounded by denying the Applicant an appeal hearing.

▶

In further deliberating on the fairness of the dismissal in all the circumstances we took account of the decision in *Iceland Frozen Foods* v *Jones* 1983 ICR 17. This case continues to be recognised in law as providing the traditionally recognised test referred to as the 'band of reasonable responses'. In other words did dismissal in the circumstances fall within the band of reasonable responses which a reasonable employer might invoke? This is an objective test as opposed to subjective. Therefore we would be erring in law if we decided this case on the basis of whether we as individuals on this panel would or would not have dismissed Mr Scoville in the circumstances. It is rather a question of what a reasonably minded person would think.

Taking account however of the evidence, this tribunal is unanimous in deciding that dismissal in the circumstances of this case was not a reasonable response to be expected of a reasonable employer. We were particularly swayed here by the evidence of Mrs Mandy Renwick, Chief Executive of Chameleon Gaming Systems, who we regarded as a credible and helpful witness. Mrs Renwick's evidence appears to clearly confirm the Applicant's version of events. We were also assisted by D.C. Clouseau's evidence which has satisfied us that there was in fact no wrongdoing on the part of Mr Scoville. Indeed D.C. Clouseau's evidence further indicates that the actual perpetrator was one of the Respondent's own partners.

This tribunal therefore finds that the Applicant was dismissed unfairly. I thereby declare that this was an unfair dismissal. The Applicant was on a gross salary of £25,000 per annum, i.e. £1,500 per month net. His immediate loss of earnings from date of dismissal until the date of this hearing therefore amount to £6,000. The Applicant remains unemployed despite having made efforts to find similar work. The tribunal hereby awards future loss of earnings for a period of a further eight months. The Respondent is therefore ordered to make a total payment accordingly to the Applicant in the sum of £18,000 within 14 days.

Claude Rumbelow
CHAIRMAN

Exercise 12 – grammar practice

REPORTED SPEECH

The following is an example of reported speech:

'Henry Moore told Charles Scoville that he was being dismissed for stealing.'

In reported speech (also known as indirect speech) we describe what was said, using different words from those actually spoken.

TASK 1

Re-phrase the following sentences to change them from direct speech into reported speech.

1. 'I've got him, the Ferrari driving swindler!'
2. 'You're dismissed as of now Scoville!'
3. 'I read an article in the local newspaper about your firm winning a case.'
4. 'I was dismissed from my job recently.'
5. 'I will try to negotiate a settlement for you.'

DIRECT SPEECH

The following is an example of direct speech:

'You are being dismissed for stealing.'

TASK 2

Write a sentence in direct speech by indicating what the speaker might actually have said in each of the following situations.

1. D.C. Clouseau asked Charles Scoville how he accounted for the Ferrari in the car-park.
2. Charles Scoville said that Henry Moore told him he was being dismissed and that he was to return his office keys immediately.
3. Charles Scoville's lawyer told him that he had a meritorious claim for unfair dismissal.
4. The Tribunal chairman said that Bannerman and Law had treated Mr Scoville reprehensibly and that he had no hesitation in declaring that Mr Scoville had been dismissed unfairly.
5. Charles Scoville said that he was pleased with the Tribunal's award of £18,000.

Law notes

Unfair dismissal

■ Employees have the right not to be unfairly dismissed, per s. 94 Employment Rights Act 1996 (ERA)
■ One year qualifying length of service required in order to be eligible to claim unfair dismissal
■ Three months limitation period for issuing claim for unfair dismissal
■ To defend an unfair dismissal claim an employer has to establish that reason for dismissal falls within one of the acceptable reasons for dismissal as provided by statute (s. 98 ERA), in particular:

1. capability (e.g. ability, skills or professional qualifications)

2. conduct

3. redundancy

4. contravention of an enactment (e.g. employee is banned from driving and employed as a delivery driver, rendering continuance of the work by that employee illegal)

5. some other substantial reason (e.g. necessary business re-organisation)

■ Employment Tribunal will then consider whether dismissal was fair or unfair in all the circumstances per s. 98(4) ERA, including for instance: whether employee was provided with opportunity of providing his or her version of events; a fair disciplinary hearing was held; employee was permitted to have a representative present; employee was provided with a right of appeal etc.

Employment Tribunal

■ Employment Tribunal (ET) is venue for unfair dismissal claims as well as for claims relating to sex, race and disability discrimination in employment. ET also has jurisdiction over claims relating to employees receiving less favourable treatment in the course of employment on the grounds of sexual orientation or religion / beliefs.

■ Appeals against ET decision must be on a point of law and submitted to the Employment Appeal Tribunal (EAT) within 42 days of ET providing its written decision.

■ Remedies ET can award for unfair dismissal include: compensation for lost earnings and loss of other benefits (e.g. health insurance, pension and use of company car etc.) and re-instatement.

■ ET can award unlimited damages in discrimination cases.

Grammar notes

Reported and direct speech

Reported speech

Verbs commonly used in reported speech include 'said', 'told' and 'explained'. Reported speech is often found in written court and tribunal decisions as well as in witness statements and press reports. (Note for instance the use of reported speech in the ET decision and witness statements you have considered in this chapter.)

There are various changes made in the course of reporting an event or comment by using reported speech. For instance:

■ Pronouns usually convert from 'I' to 'he' / 'she' and 'my' converts to 'his' / 'her'
■ 'Tomorrow' becomes 'the following day' / 'yesterday' becomes 'the previous day'.
■ Tenses change so that:

1. the present becomes the past

2. the present perfect becomes the past perfect

3. the past simple becomes the past perfect

■ Modal verbs change so that you often find for instance that: 'can' becomes 'could'; 'will' becomes 'would'; 'may' becomes 'might'.

■ There are seven main verb structures with reported speech:

1. verb + 'that'   ('He said that he was leaving')

2. verb + object + that   ('He told us that he was leaving')

3. verb + 'that' + 'should' + bare infinitive   ('She told us that we should leave')

4. verb + infinitive   ('He said he tried to arrive on time')

5. verb + objective + infinitive   ('He told me to go')

6. verb + 'ing'   ('He said he liked working')

7. verb + gerund   ('He reported seeing the driver stop suddenly')

Direct speech
When writing in direct speech we repeat what was actually stated, placing those words in quotation marks ('   '). The legal term 'verbatim' means that the written document being referred to recites the actual words of the speaker. It is important for a lawyer to know whether the words he is reading are 'verbatim' since the precise words spoken by a party are often of crucial importance in determining the outcome of a case. (E.g. in a breach of contract case, what exactly did the seller of a motor vehicle say about the condition of the vehicle?)

PART 3
Law bulletin

Chapter 11   Law bulletin

Learning Objectives

This chapter contains a selection of articles on topical legal issues. By completing the tasks in this chapter you will have:

■ Read and considered an article on the distinction between barristers and solicitors
■ Read and considered an article on witness examination in the courtroom
■ Read and considered an article on the Asian legal market
■ Read and considered an article on international litigation
■ Practised relevant grammar exercises including tense review and comparative and superlative forms of written and spoken English

Text 1 – solicitor or barrister?

Read the following article then complete the exercises which follow.

WHICH ROUTE – SOLICITOR OR BARRISTER?

Many students have decided on a career in the law, but are unsure of the next step. Margot Taylor **explains the pros and cons of each branch of the profession**

The two main branches of the legal profession are solicitors and barristers (advocates in Scotland). There are also legal executives, who regard themselves as a third branch. In the past ten years, the difference between the branches has become increasingly blurred: solicitors can now qualify as higher court advocates, and barristers can deal directly with some kinds of client (chiefly other professionals) without the need for the client to see a solicitor first.

TYPE AND VARIETY OF WORK

Solicitors' work covers a broad range, including advising commercial and private clients on business matters and property and undertaking litigation. The degree of specialisation of solicitors' firms varies enormously. Some offer general legal services, from conveyancing and drafting wills to acting for defendants in criminal cases. Others specialise in one or two areas, perhaps doing only corporate work or personal injury work. The smaller the firm and the broader its range of work, the less likely its solicitors will specialise in only one area.

Most barristers' work is confined to litigation, although some do largely advisory work, for example on taxation or company matters. Traditionally barristers specialise in one or a few areas of law, although this is not true of all. In their early years most undertake a broad range of cases until they develop expertise in a particular area. Some barristers in "general common law" chambers continue to have a broadly based practice. Whether, or how much, you specialise as a barrister will depend to a large extent on the cases you get in your early years.

So, if you do not want to do litigation, think twice before you become a barrister. Otherwise, whether or not you specialise will not rest entirely on whether or not you join the Bar or become a solicitor but will be influenced by the type of firm or chambers you join.

TRAINING

Beyond the academic stage the training to become a barrister or solicitor is very different. The Bar Vocational Course is exclusively focused on the skills and knowledge required of an advocate: litigation evidence drafting advocacy, etc. This is followed by 12 months of pupilage. The Legal Practice Course is much broader and covers business law and practice, property and litigation and advocacy. This is followed by a two-year training contract in a firm.

WORKING CONDITIONS

Most solicitors are salaried employees and keep office hours, report to a senior person and work within the collective ethos of the firm. However, they generally have "billing targets" (to achieve a number of chargeable hours) which can be stressful and require detailed record-keeping. Barristers are self-employed but usually work out of chambers (a group of barristers) with a clerk who takes referrals from solicitors. Theoretically free to work as and when they please barristers must be available to take work as it comes in. Barristers are generally paid a fee for each piece of work from which they must deduct their share of the costs of running the chambers. A barrister's earnings are therefore much less secure than a solicitor's, particularly in the early years.

ADVOCACY

Many barristers, particularly those doing criminal work, spend most of their time as advocates. However, some civil practitioners spend more of their time dealing with cases out of court. Solicitors have rights of audience in the lower courts and although many do no advocacy some do a substantial amount.

Some solicitors qualify for rights of audience in the higher courts, with some City firms encouraging this. The advantage of this route over qualifying as a barrister is that you work from the base of a legal practice. It is done to enhance your work. The disadvantage is that you are unlikely to do the same volume of advocacy as those who qualify for the Bar. If you really only want to do advocacy, the Bar, particularly criminal work, is probably the place for you.

CONTACT WITH CLIENTS

A solicitor has overall conduct of a case and develops a working relationship with the client, which can be rewarding. But it can also be frustrating, particularly dealing with the more demanding clients, accounting for all client money and dealing with documentation and costs. A barrister is briefed by the solicitor for specific tasks, for example, drafting a document or acting as an advocate. This would appeal to someone who dislikes routine paperwork but can be frustrating if insufficient or wrong information is provided. A barrister may have little opportunity to develop any relationship with the client.

NOT A FINAL CHOICE

The division between solicitors and barristers is becoming less distinct, with solicitors doing more advocacy and clients instructing barristers directly. Moving between the two halves of the profession is straightforward, so a choice now will not dictate your work for life.

Margot Taylor, Principal Lecturer, Inns of Court School of Law: *The Times*, 20 January 2004, Student Law, p. 11.

Exercise 1 – comprehension

Answer the following questions concerning the above article.

1. Explain in a few sentences the main difference between a barrister's work and that of a solicitor.

2. How long does a trainee barrister's pupillage last?

3. How long does a trainee solicitor's training contract last?

4. Which branch of the legal profession developes a closer on-going relationship with clients and why?

5. State two areas of law which solicitors can specialise in.

6. What factors influence the areas of legal work a barrister becomes involved in during the initial stage of his or her career?

7. Where do barristers practise from?

8. Which branch of the legal profession do you consider yourself best suited to and why? Discuss.

Exercise 2 – word search

Complete the following sentences by filling in the blank spaces with appropriate phrases from the text.

1. Barristers' work predominantly involves [1] _____ , i.e. court work.

2. There are basically two types of lawyers in England, namely solicitors and [2] _____ .

3. Solicitors are often under pressure to achieve [3] _____ _____ .

4. Barristers undertake a [4] _____ _____ course following the academic stage of their training.

5. Solicitors undertake a [5] _____ _____ course following the academic stage of their training.

6. Solicitors have overall conduct of a case whereas barristers are [6] _____ at specific stages of a case.

Text 2 – techniques for cross-examining a witness in court

Read the following article then complete the exercises which follow.

HAVING CROSS WORDS IN THE COURTROOM

Q How do you start to prepare for cross-examination?

A Practitioners prepare for cross-examination differently. Some start with the witness statement (which stands as, in most civil cases, the evidence in chief). They then work through the points the witness supports in the other side's case, take out a list of other issues that need to be challenged, mark any internal inconsistencies in the witness statement, explore the trial bundle for documents to put to the witness, and work out a series of questions from there.

A better approach is to start from the propositions you would like to make in the closing submissions – and work backwards. Sometimes arguments are raised in closing submissions that have not been put to the witnesses during cross-examination. This is unavoidable as cases change considerably during trial. However, more often, it is because the themes of the witnesses' evidence had not been tied in to the closing arguments beforehand. Alert judges are aware of this. How often have you heard in judgments 'XYZ was not put to the witness, so I am unable to make a finding on that...' or 'counsel chose not to challenge that in evidence...' Sometimes the failure to challenge is deliberate; often it is not. You can reduce the risk of this happening by tying in, from the start, the themes of your cross-examination with the bare threads of your closing argument.

An effective way to start your preparation is to consider from the outset the theme your series of questions is going to follow. The theme will be case-specific, designed to deal with your client's slant on a particular issue that the judge must consider when reaching his decision. Equally, your theme may be based solely on discrediting the testimony of the witness. Either way, this theme should be prevalent throughout your questioning.

Set out your theme on a cross-examination 'route plan' – an overall guide to your cross-examination from where all your notes and questions will be devised. Only once this is prepared are you ready to start effectively preparing your cross-examination.

Q How should I approach my cross-examination route plan?

A Your route plan is the guide to where you want to take this witness in front of the judge (or jury in criminal cases). The purpose of any cross-examination is twofold: to elicit favourable evidence and discredit evidence that is unhelpful. Anything else is a fishing exercise, which should be avoided. Set out the following on a sheet of paper:

- Which part of this witness's evidence in chief assists or supports your case? Usually there are a few agreed facts – make a list of these.
- How can this witness corroborate your theory of the case? Tie these agreed facts in with your theory of the case and consider the propositions required to turn this witness into corroborating your client's slant on the issues.
- What must this witness admit? Make a list of the propositions you would like this witness to admit – these propositions should all tie in with your theme for this witness and the overall theory of the case in closing.
- What should the witness admit? Consider what the witness cannot deny from the agreed facts – the propositions from which he cannot possibly escape. Use these to develop your position in other areas. These are all useful tools for effective cross-examination.

Q What tips can you give practitioners in advance of their first cross-examinations?

A Cross-examination depends on your audience. You are expected to act in a different way before juries or lay magistrates than you are in front of a county or High Court judge or a lawyer-led tribunal. Remember who your audience is and be flexible. On presentation, it is usually a good idea to bear in mind the following advice:

- Make your questions leading – answers should be yes or no. If you ask an open question, the witness can respond in any number of ways.
- Make a statement of fact and ask the witness to agree with it. The best practitioners keep control of their witnesses by putting facts to the witness in the question and asking them 'do you agree?' This leaves the witness with no room to manoeuvre into unhelpful matters. Lead up gently to the main question with a series of agreed facts from your route plan.
- Be confident. Advocacy is like acting – and even more so in jury trials. If you do not project *gravitas* and authority the effect of your cross-examination will be lost, a jury will not be impressed and the witness will start to take advantage.
- Be polite to the independent and expert witness, unless circumstances dictate otherwise.
- Listen to the witness. Often cross-examiners are not listening to the witness. This is acceptable if the witness provides you with an expected answer, but witnesses are more often than not sophisticated and unpredictable. Listen to what they are saying and be prepared to challenge an issue they raise for the first time.
- Do not, under any circumstances, argue with the witness. All too often cross-examiners respond to throwaway remarks by witnesses designed to challenge propositions put to them. If they answer a question with a question, tell them it is your role to ask the questions and their role to answer them.

  On content, remember:

- Make your strongest points at the start and end of your cross-examination.
- Keep your eye on your audience; judge the reactions. You may not need the audience's constant attention – you may, after all, be eliciting evidence for a closing submission – but you do need to keep its interest or provide for it a point of reference if you want the audience to follow your theme on closing.

- Vary the order of subject matter. This may be better done by taking it issue-by-issue or chronologically.
- Try your best not to allow the witness to repeat his direct examination.
- Know the probable answer to each question – and devise a route plan for any unexpected answers.
- Do not start to prepare a script of all the questions you propose to ask. It may make you feel safer having all the questions on one sheet of paper, but it will not help you on the day.

This column was written by Justin Michaelson (Weil, Gotshal & Manges) on behalf of the Solicitors' Association of Higher Court Advocates (SAHCA): *Gazette*, Vol. 101, No. 13, 1 April 2004, p. 6.

Exercise 3 – word collocations

Match each word from the first column below with a corresponding word in the second column. By way of example the first one is done for you.

witness		question
open		trial
cross		examination
jury		statement
High		chief
examination in		Court

Exercise 4 – word search

Complete each blank space below by inserting a word or phrase from the text which is similar in meaning to each of the following. (The paragraph number of the text in which the answer is located is indicated in brackets to assist you.)

1. closing submissions   c _ _ _ _ _ _ _ _ _ _ _ s (para. 2)

2. contentions   p _ _ _ _ _ _ _ _ _ _ _ (para. 2)

3. witnesses' version of events   witnesses' e _ _ _ _ _ _ _ (para. 2)

4. backs up your legal arguments   s _ _ _ _ _ _ _ your c _ _ _ (para. 5)

5. court representation   a _ _ _ _ _ _ _ (para. 6)

6. advocates who question other party's witnesses   c _ _ _ _ e _ _ _ _ _ _ _ _ (para. 6)

Text 3 – the Asian legal market

Read the following text then complete the exercises which follow.

ASIAN TIGERS PREPARE TO SPRING

AFTER A DECADE OF ECONOMIC TURMOIL, ASIA IS BUZZING. WHILE SOME LAW FIRMS ARE CAUTIOUS ABOUT HAVING A PRESENCE THERE, MANY WANT TO TAKE ADVANTAGE OF RISING INVESTMENT, SAYS LUCY HICKMAN

Economically speaking, Asia has had a hard time over the past few years. Deep recession lasting nearly a decade for most Asian countries – including former linchpins Hong Kong and Japan – political unrest for many, and then the SARS virus provided the poisoned icing on the cake. All of this, of course, has affected lawyers.

Most international law firms with Asian offices have dug in deep to weather the storm, often redeploying fee-earners when the worst-struck practice areas – finance and corporate – hit rock bottom. As Don Kelly, Lovells' regional managing partner for Asia, says: 'Staffing issues are an ongoing challenge. We do the best we can. Fortunately, our people tend to be pretty flexible.

'Our Vietnam office – which we have had for ten years – is a good example of this. In the early years, there was lots of intellectual property and project work in the region, so we kept it staffed up all the time. Then things went a bit quiet, so we ran the office on a fly-in, fly-out basis. There's a sense of revival again now and we make sure there's always a Lovells lawyer sitting in that office. It just won't always be the same lawyer or from the same practice area.'

With the economy and therefore the legal work in Japan and Hong Kong showing definite signs of improvement, and China positively booming, it seems the law firms' patience may be paying off.

Paul Browne, a Tokyo-based finance partner with Simmons & Simmons, says: 'Japan is the world's second biggest economy but it's been suffering in recession for ten years or so. However, there are definitely signs of improvement in Japan – and in other parts of Asia too – and people are generally cautiously optimistic. We're seeing increasing investment, which has a knock-on effect on the requirement for lawyers.'

A strange time then, perhaps, for Denton Wilde Sapte (DWS) to disband its Asian practice, closing offices in Hong Kong, Beijing, Tokyo and Singapore, in a move affecting 12 partners and around 100 staff in total. The withdrawal follows on from the firm's strategy review, which was launched 18 months ago in a bid to bolster profits (see [2004] *Gazette*, 16 April, 6).

DWS declined to be interviewed by the *Gazette*, but on announcing the closures last month, chairman James Dallas said the Asian practice was not strategically necessary for the sector groups on which the firm now wants to focus: energy, infrastructure and transport; financial services; real estate; and technology, media and telecommunications.

'We have concluded that we should withdraw from Asia and direct more resources to areas with stronger client demand, including Europe, the Middle East, and elsewhere,' he said in a statement.

Meanwhile, Freshfields Bruckhaus Deringer is also poised to close its three-partner Bangkok office, which has a total staff of 81. It has already downsized its operations in Singapore, not replacing staff when they leave.

Mr Kelly says that DWS's withdrawal from Asia was on the cards, with numerous CVs from DWS lawyers flying around before the announcement. However, he finds Freshfields' retreat from Bangkok more puzzling.

'It's a strange time to be pulling out of Asia. It's been very tough over the last three years, but recently we have seen definite signs of improvement. Firms that have been here throughout the hard period will have spent a lot of time, money and effort, and now is the time they may be seeing some return on that investment.'

Most agree though that south-east Asia is a hard market to crack. As Ashurst's Japanese group head, Alan Kitchin, says: 'South-east Asia is very difficult. It's very competitive on fees. You tend to be acting more for the [local] law firms than for the banks in that region, so it's hard to keep the rates up. Firms in there are really struggling.'

Wong Kien Keong, Baker & McKenzie's Asia-Pacific chairman, adds: 'Well-known firms have folded up their operations in some major money-centre jurisdictions like Hong Kong and Singapore, while larger domestic firms are getting some cross-border work which eats into the pie of the international firms.

The quality of domestic firms is also improving, particularly in Hong Kong, China, Bangkok and Singapore.

'The least lucrative market continues to be Manila among the countries which receive significant foreign direct investment. Other countries on the fringe in Asia will continue to suffer, like Myanmar, Laos and Cambodia,' he predicts. These are all countries where no UK firm has set up.

Perry Noble, Freshfields' managing partner in Asia, says: 'The economic conditions in south-east Asia have been pretty tough. There was the economic crisis at the end of the 1990s, then the technology boom died out and there has been a lot of political unrest.

'We have taken the decision to withdraw from the Bangkok market, or we are at least considering it in principle. From my point of view, no one makes any money in that part of Asia and I have a responsibility to the partners to get the best return on their investment.'

He says the economic conditions recently have made the decision about where to invest more difficult. 'It's not necessarily that I believe there will be no growth in south-east Asia – it probably is improving – but the prospects don't justify that level of investment.'

Since 1997, Lovells has had an office in Singapore which acts as a hub, handling work throughout south-east Asia.

Mr Kelly says his firm is considering a series of strategic alliances in the regions, which should open up the local markets without the financial risk of opening offices in jurisdictions such as Thailand and Indonesia.

'It may well be that we will be looking to do more with local firms. We would like to have more presence there but short of opening a new office. It remains difficult around there,' he says.

Lovells' director of international projects, Marc Bartel, adds: 'There is a buzz about some parts of the region, but you might have a flavour of the month with people looking to revive deals in one place, then, because of a bit of political instability, the focus changes. We are keeping our ears to the ground on this one.'

Ashurst, which has offices in Singapore and Tokyo, has no intention of pulling out of Asia.

Mr Kitchin explains that, as the Asian market generates an enormous amount of work for its other offices, including London, and that at least three of Ashurst's top 20 clients are Japanese, the firm is planning to expand its Asian operations.

He says: 'We are looking at China. We have never merged; we like to do things our-selves and every year we open a new office. We don't want to compromise our quality by being all over the place for the sake of it, but China is a difficult market not to be in because so many clients want to do business there.'

Since its 2001 entry to the World Trade Organisation, China has become one of the world's fastest-moving economies, with year-on-year growth of gross domestic prod-uct at 8%, foreign direct investment (FDI) at 57%, foreign trade at 40% and industrial output at 17%. Law firms not yet established there want to be, and those already there are looking to expand – with the obvious exception of DWS.

With the opening up of international trade, and massive inward investment, foreign investors are attracted to what they see as a largely untapped market and a low manu-facturing cost base.

The Chinese government's push to transform the energy markets has rejuvenated the sector, while the liberalisation of the Chinese banking system allows foreign banks to provide local currency business to Chinese clients. And since the business and regula-tory environment is not as developed as in more sophisticated markets, there is also a need for lawyers to advise not just on expansion and investment but also on restructur-ing and reorganisation.

Mr Keong says: 'The most lucrative Asian legal market remains China. It has the highest amount of FDI in the world. The Chinese legal market is possibly one of the largest in the world, because it requires a great deal of financial and legal skills to lift its economic standard to a level closer to the developed world.'

Michael Liu, head of Allen & Overy's Asian corporate group, says that to gain a firm foothold in the Chinese market, one must not look at China as being independent from Hong Kong – sovereignty of which was handed back to the Chinese by the British seven years ago.

'We need to think of our Chinese practice as one team in three locations. Beijing is the government seat, and Shanghai and Hong Kong are the major commercial centres. You need full service capability in all three cities to cover the Chinese market effectively.

'Hong Kong remains a key world financial and business centre, but it is now just one piece of a bigger jigsaw.'

The firm's head of Asia practice, Brian Harrison, says: 'As our clients are stepping up their presence in the Chinese mainland market, we will follow suit and further expand our presence there. On the other hand, there are also business opportunities to serve the needs of Chinese companies which are revitalising in preparation for further mar-ket competition. So the timing is ripe for us.'

Freshfields has had offices in Beijing and Shanghai since 1993, and Mr Noble says China is an important part of the firm's plans.

He says that 75% of the work done by the firm's 18-partner Hong Kong office has a Chinese connection.

'China has been important for all businesses in Hong Kong. SARS didn't help and Hong Kong has been dire for a long time, but the work coming from China has been a real relief for everybody.

'Hong Kong is a small market and ever since its return to China, the economic condi-tions have been poor. Combine that with the fact the area is massively over-lawyered and you get everyone cutting each other's throats on the price of work. It has been very tough.'

What could escalate the Asian legal market's revival are plans by the Japanese and South Korean governments to allow foreign law firms to form full partnerships with – and also employ – local lawyers. It is expected that the restrictions will be lifted next year, says Mr Browne.

'Deregulation will improve things. We have a joint venture with a big Japanese law firm and to them the prospect of deregulation is an exciting one because they are very international in their outlook. At the moment though, we are not considering a full partnership. We are very happy with the model we have got,' he says.

Mr Kelly says rumours are rife of plans by English law firms to merge with Japanese firms – although he declines to name names.

For Lovells though, a full merger is not on the cards, with the firm preferring to introduce local talent on a lateral-hire basis.

'We want Japanese law capability but cherry-picking individuals is certainly where we would like to start. Then we will see how it goes.'

In south-east Asia, the cautious approach of retreating firms like DWS has yet to be weighed against the go-getting strategies of others. But given the speed of developments in the region, it should not be too long before the winning strategy reveals itself.

Lucy Hickman, freelance journalist: *Gazette*, Vol. 101, No. 20, 20 May 2004, pp. 24–7.

Exercise 5 – comprehension

1. Which areas of legal practice have been most adversely affected throughout Asia as a result of recession?

2. Which country has the second largest economy?

3. In which country is demand for legal work 'booming'?

4. Name an Asian country in which no UK law firm has set up.

5. What does 'FDI' stand for?

6. What are foreign law firms likely to be able to do in the near future which could assist in reviving the Asian legal market?

Exercise 6 – vocabulary

Find alternative words or phrases from the text meaning the same as the following.

1. transitory basis (para. 3)

2. thriving (para. 4)

3. plan (para. 6)

4. retreat (para. 8)

5. reduced (para. 9)

6. likely (para. 10)

Exercise 7 – tenses

Complete the following sentences by putting the verbs in brackets into the correct tense forms.

1. Since 2001 China's economy [1] _____ (develop) fast.

2. The partners [2] _____ (meet) at 3.00 pm last Friday.

3. Several law firms have [3] _____ (open) offices in Beijing recently.

4. At least one law firm has recently [4] _____ (closing) an office in Singapore.

5. Demand for legal work in Hong Kong is [5] _____ (show) signs of improvement.

6. The Chinese legal market is [6] _____ (provide) increasing work for foreign law firms.

Exercise 8 – idioms

Written and spoken English commonly includes expressions (idioms) which are intended to convey a meaning other than the literal interpretation. There are a number of examples of idioms within the text. For example: '... the SARS virus provided the poisoned icing on the cake'. The words 'poisoned icing' are in fact used to relate to the reader that the SARS virus was a further factor contributing to recession in Asian markets rather than having anything to do with actual icing on a cake!

TASK 1

Match each of the expressions in the first column below with its corresponding meaning in the second column. By way of illustration the first one is done for you.

weather the storm	reduced
hit rock bottom	difficult market to enter
on the cards	monitor events
downsized	survive a difficult situation
hard market to crack	currently popular
ear to the ground	likely to happen
flavour of the month	to be at the lowest point

TASK 2

Now complete the following sentences by filling each of the gaps with an appropriate idiom from the panel below.

bury the hatchet	on the grapevine	redtape
Scot free	raining cats and dogs	eager beaver

1. I have heard _____ that he has been appointed as a Judge.

2. It became cloudy and started _____ .

3. The Defendant got off _____ .

4. The new lawyer works very hard, he's an _____ .

5. They stopped arguing and agreed to _____ .

6. The civil service is sometimes said to be full of _____ .

Exercise 9 – comparatives and superlatives

There are a number of examples of comparatives and superlatives in the text. The following are examples of superlatives:

'... the *worst-struck* practice areas ...' and 'We do the *best* we can'.

TASK 1

Use the superlatives from the box below to complete the following phrases.

fastest	highest	most	least

1. China has the _____ amount of foreign domestic investment (FDI) in the world.

2. The _____ lucrative market is Manila.

3. The _____ lucrative market is China.

4. China has become one of the world's _____ moving economies.

The following is an example of a comparative:

'Resources should be directed to areas with *stronger* client demand.'

TASK 2

Use the comparatives from the box below to complete the following sentences. (Note that some words in the box may be required more than once whereas others may not be required.)

more	bigger	stronger	closer

1. Hong Kong is part of a _____ jigsaw.

2. Economic conditions have made decisions about where to invest _____ difficult.

3. The business and regulatory environment is _____ developed within sophisticated markets.

4. Some law firms are directing resources to areas with _____ client demand.

Note that 'as' can be used to compare two similars. E.g. 'Tokyo is as expensive as London.' It can also be used negatively. E.g. 'Regional law firms don't usually have as many branch offices as the larger city firms.'

Text 4 – international litigation

Read the following text then complete the exercises which follow.

SHOPPING AROUND

THE ALLURE OF SUBSTANTIAL DAMAGES HAS PROMPTED MANY CLAIMANTS TO SCOUR THE GLOBE FOR THE MOST ADVANTAGEOUS ARENA IN WHICH TO FIGHT THEIR LEGAL BATTLES, REPORTS NIGEL HANSON

Contingency fees, jury trials for all civil cases and the chance to win substantial punitive damages are just some of the advantages of litigating in the US

As globalisation shrinks the world, lawyers are increasingly shopping around for the best forum for their clients' litigation. Claimants who play their cards right can scoop greater damages, while expense and frustration await those unaware of the vagaries of international law.

City solicitors say the recent collapse of multinationals, such as Italian dairy giant Parmalat, has created opportunities, particularly for US firms, as global investors scramble to protect their interests – usually by joining class actions in the US.

Meanwhile, the recent decision in *David Van Der Velde (deceased) v Philip Morris* has driven home the limitations of forum shopping for individual litigants (see [2004] *Gazette*, 5 February, 6).

The claim was brought by Gabriella Van Der Velde, whose husband's illness and death were allegedly caused by smoking cigarettes manufactured and sold by US tobacco company Philip Morris.

Although her husband lived all his life in England, she tried to sue in the US, where higher damages are available.

A New York district court decided that the US was not the appropriate jurisdiction – *forum non conveniens* – because England had the 'most significant factual relationship' to the litigation. Her shopping sortie failed, but it highlighted the trend for seeking an ideal forum abroad.

Adam Johnson, a litigation partner at City firm Herbert Smith, says the US has long been considered a favourable forum for claimants, particularly in personal injury (PI) cases.

Contingency fees, jury trials for all civil cases and the chance to win substantial punitive damages – often awarded as multiples of any compensatory damages – are just some of the advantages.

In addition, US discovery rules give claimants wider pre-trial disclosure, increasing pressure on defendants to settle.

Mr Johnson says: 'In the US, you have to give full disclosure of documents and oral discovery for witnesses through depositions.

'All potentially relevant witnesses are subjected to extensive cross-examination by the claimant's lawyers to fish around for evidence that might be relevant. All these things make litigation in the US very attractive for claimants and very unattractive for defendants, and this is what gives rise to forum shopping.'

Conversely, he says Italy is often considered a good place to defend a case because bureaucratic delays may postpone the outcome for years.

Mr Johnson says more forum shopping has emerged in the wake of the financial crises engulfing Enron, Worldcom and Parmalat.

US law firms such as Milberg Weiss now specialise in securities claims on behalf of disgruntled investors. 'They will set up class actions, typically brought in New York, and invite investors from around the world to join in,' says Mr Johnson. 'Effectively, it's inviting people to forum-shop in America.'

Jeremy Sharman, a litigation partner at London-based intellectual property specialists Bird & Bird, says forum shopping can deliver specific procedural advantages.

He explains: 'In some countries, there's no obligation to produce any damaging documents. That's completely different from the UK. It may have an impact in cases where you didn't want certain documents to come to light.'

Defamation is a growth area for the cross-border shoppers. Dan Tench, a partner in the media litigation department at London firm Olswang, says the recent proliferation in international claims is largely the result of the impact of Internet publishing, combined with political developments such as the 11 September 2001 terrorist attacks in the US and the fragmentation of the former Soviet Union.

The case of *Gutnick v Dow Jones & Co* (see [2003] *Gazette*, 25 April, 6) confirmed that a businessman allegedly defamed in an article published by the *Wall Street Journal* online was allowed to take proceedings in Australia against the Web site's US-based publisher, Dow Jones, because several of the Web site's subscribers lived there.

In addition to the impetus from Internet cases, the press has recently published allegedly defamatory stories linking prominent Arabs with al-Qaeda, and Russian businessmen with corruption and arms dealing.

Many such cases, says Mr Tench, have been litigated in London because, in contrast with PI, England is a better forum for defamation claims than most others, notably the US.

Moreover, many of the world's newspapers are published in London, providing a necessary jurisdictional connection.

Suing for defamation in the US is notoriously difficult because defendants are protected by the first amendment of the US constitution – which protects free speech – and the so-called Sullivan defence, which requires public figures to prove actual malice.

Mr Tench says: 'These are the factors that are driving the international claim. Our regime in England and Wales is still pretty favourable to claimants. We don't have the broad, "public figure" defence.

'I think people also feel there is perhaps more reliability or predictability here than in some other jurisdictions, such as France.'

But Mr Tench adds that while libel clients are flocking to London, they need to be sure that any judgment obtained will be enforceable where it matters.

'There is no point in being able to bring a defamation case in England but not being able to get enforcement abroad,' he says.

In a case in 1995, a US court in Maryland reviewed sceptically the development of English libel law down the centuries before refusing to enforce a defamation judgment obtained in London on policy grounds. Mr Tench says it shows US judges' 'uneasiness' about English law's comparatively pro-claimant approach.

Forum shopping also pays dividends in intellectual property (IP) cases.

Until about 2010, when it is expected that a unified European Union (EU) patent system will be introduced, the EU's treatment of patents looks set to remain fragmented. Clive Thorne, an IP partner at City firm Denton Wilde Sapte, says that under the existing European patent convention, each EU member state's approach to patent litigation is different.

'The interesting thing is that courts in each member state of the EU jurisdiction can, and do, reach different decisions on the validity of a patent,' he says.

Differences also arise over cost, speed and remedies. 'Germany is very expensive – you have to pay a very significant court fee up front,' Mr Thorne says. 'Some say the UK is expensive, but I'm not convinced. Reforms brought in by the patent judges have got it running very smoothly and efficiently, although it is perhaps a little more expensive litigating here than in Holland.'

Dutch courts are far more likely than others to grant wide-reaching injunctive relief, intended to be enforceable in other jurisdictions.

Gill Doran, head of family law at City firm Withers, says choice of jurisdiction can affect a financial settlement following divorce. Scandinavian countries, for example, have no concept of spousal maintenance.

Ms Doran says: 'I can think of one example where a husband definitely started proceedings in Sweden because that was a favourable jurisdiction to him compared with England, where maintenance is payable.'

Pre-empting the other side by starting proceedings in a chosen forum can be a decisive factor, particularly since the implementation of a convention known widely as 'Brussels II', which requires the court first seized of certain actions to try them to the exclusion of others.

Many clients would be unaware, Ms Doran adds, that a pre-nuptial agreement signed in New York has full force there but would be given much less weight in England should the couple emigrate.

'Forum shopping can make a huge difference,' she says. 'Normally, it has to be thought about a long way ahead to get the most advantage. It often requires someone going home for some period of time to fulfil the requirements and benefits of their own jurisdiction.

'It sounds incredibly calculated, but it is jurisdiction shopping – or jurisdiction planning.'

However, tactical awareness can mean the difference between keeping and losing children. Marcus Dearle, another partner at Withers, says potential surrogate mothers who visit California are often 'blissfully ignorant' that their surrogacy contract will be fully binding there and they can be forced to give up the child they are carrying by the courts.

In England and Wales, however, a surrogate mother who wants to keep the baby immediately after giving birth is likely to be allowed to do so.

Forum shopping, in brief, is something nobody can afford to overlook. As Mr Dearle says: 'It is potentially big business. Savings or gains amounting to millions of pounds can be made. Modern telecommunications, globalisation and cheaper travel have made the world a much smaller place.

'Lawyers and their clients will increasingly need to be internationally aware of the concept in the 21st century.'

Nigel Hanson: *Gazette*, Vol. 101, No. 9, 4 March 2004, pp. 10–11.

Exercise 10 – gerunds and infinitives

The infinitive is the basic form of a verb. A gerund is usually a verb used as a noun ending in 'ing'.

Verbs which can be followed by infinitives include:

afford	agree	appear	arrange	ask	attempt	begin	choose
dare	decide	expect	fail	forget	happen	intend	manage
neglect	offer	prepare	pretend	promise	refuse		

Verbs which can be followed by the gerund 'ing' form include:

admit	avoid	consider	delay	detest	dislike	endure	enjoy
escape	finish	forgive	imagine	mention	resist	suggest	understand

Verbs which can be followed by either gerunds or infinitives include:

like	love	hate	prefer	continue	try

Complete the following summary of the text by inserting in each blank space the appropriate gerund or infinitive form of the words in brackets.

TEXT SUMMARY

Lawyers now consider [1] _____ (shop around) when [2] _____ (deal) with litigation cases. They are sometimes provided with a choice as to which country [3] _____ (take) a case to. Solicitors sometimes suggest for instance [4] _____ (bring) a class action in New York. Solicitors usually prefer however to [5] _____ (starting) a defamation case in the UK because [6] _____ (sue) for defamation in the US is usually more difficult.

Exercise 11 – discourse markers

Discourse markers are used to connect sentences and to indicate additional information. Legal English uses a number of discourse markers in this way with words such as: 'moreover'; 'furthermore'; 'further or alternatively' etc.

Discourse markers can usually be placed in various positions within a sentence and can be used for a variety of specific purposes, including to: focus the reader on a particular issue, contrast issues or ideas, provide emphasis or to structure information.

There are a significant number of examples of discourse markers being used in these ways throughout the text. For instance:

■ Cause and effect: 'As globalisation shrinks the world, lawyers are increasingly shopping around ...'
■ Contrast: 'Although her husband lived all his life in England, she tried to sue in the US ...'
■ Addition: 'In addition, US discovery rules give Claimants wider pre-trial disclosure ...'

Further typical discourse markers in legal English include:

■ *with reference to*; *regarding*; *as regards*   (for focusing and linking)
■ *firstly*; *to begin with*; *finally*   (for structuring)
■ *as a result*; *therefore*; *consequently*   (for sequencing in a logical order)

Complete the following sentences by selecting appropriate discourse markers from the panel below.

1. _____ it is hereby agreed that this amount will be in full and final settlement.

2. _____ I would like to introduce the main speaker.

3. It will not be necessary _____ to take this matter any further.

4. The Claimant is a wealthy man _____ of the damages awarded to him.

5. Damages awards are usually higher in US courts. _____ it may be more convenient to issue legal proceedings in England.

6. He is a good barrister. He is not popular _____ with colleagues in chambers.

however	as a result	to begin with / firstly
therefore	furthermore	on the other hand

Exercise 12 – discussion

INDIVIDUAL EXERCISE

1. If you are working on your own, prepare a short letter of advice to a client explaining the main issues to be considered when deciding which country to commence legal proceedings in.

2. Read the Group Exercise below. Write an opinion on the four issues indicated by bullet-points. Discuss this opinion with a colleague or friend.

GROUP EXERCISE

1. Work in pairs, discussing your views and opinions on the relative merits and disadvantages of the UK and US court systems. Consider for instance issues such as:

■ Should US courts continue to award very large punitive awards (some of which amount to billions of dollars). Are these awards in the public interest?
■ Should English courts award punitive damages?

▶

■ Is it right that individuals should be able to 'shop around' internationally to find the most financially advantageous legal jurisdiction in which to bring their claims?

■ Should contingency fees (arrangements whereby a lawyer works on a no win–no fee basis and takes a percentage of the damages, often 25%, if the claim is successful) be permitted?

2. Prepare and make a presentation either individually or in pairs to the rest of your group on 'The future of international litigation'. (Address issues such as whether you think that issuing court proceedings in other countries will become an increasing trend, which areas of legal practice will be most affected and why.)

Appendix 1
Study and research guide

Throughout this book you have been presented with legal and linguistic skills practice, including in reading, writing, drafting and advocacy. Such practice should assist in developing your competence in using legal English both in legal study and in legal practice. The purpose of this section of the book is to provide you with a further appreciation of the *sources* of law and their relative importance. Certain features of the *text* of law and where to locate it will also be considered.

Sources of United Kingdom law

Legislation

United Kingdom (UK) law is primarily created by legislation. The sources of legislation are:

European Union legislation

Legislation enacted by or delegated by the UK Parliament

The ultimate source of UK law is now legislation created by the European Union. The UK largely lost 'sovereignty' over its law-making process as a result of becoming a signatory to the European Union (previously known as the European Community) on 1 January 1973. In particular, the UK Parliament granted overriding law-making authority to the European Union by enacting the European Communities Act 1972. The EU has its own Parliament, its Secretariat being based in Luxembourg, committee meetings usually being held in Brussels.

European Union law

Primary European Union (EU) law consists mainly of treaties. Rights provided under primary EU law are directly enforceable through UK courts if domestic law does not specifically grant those rights.

Secondary EU law takes the form of:

■ Regulations: a Regulation is entirely binding upon the UK as a member state of the EU. It is directly applicable in UK law without the need for the UK Parliament to enact the regulation through domestic legislation. Regulations are directly applicable, both against the state (known as being directly applicable) and against individuals and companies (known as being horizontally applicable). An example of a Regulation is the free movement of workers within the EU regulation.

149

- Directives: a Directive imposes a binding duty on member states to implement the provisions contained within the Directive. A Directive is not however directly imposed. Instead, the member state is responsible for determining the form and method by which to implement the provisions of the Directive into its domestic law. A Directive is said to have 'vertical effect' since it 'directs' a member state to incorporate the Directive into its own law.

- Decisions: these are binding and include decisions from:

    (a) The Commission (based in Brussels, consisting of 'commissioners' and which represents the EU as a whole)

    (b) Decisions of the European Court of Justice (ECJ) based in Luxembourg (e.g. decisions in competition law cases)

- Recommendations and Opinions: issued by the Commission or the Council (consisting of Ministers from member states and which adopts legislation proposed by the Commission). Such Recommendations and Opinions are persuasive in nature rather than binding. (The ECJ adjudicates on disputes between member states relating to alleged violations of treaties as well as making rulings on the correct interpretation of EU legislation.)

English (UK) law

UK legislation is created by the UK Parliament (Parliament). This legislation is in the form of 'statutes', also known as 'Acts of Parliament'. There is in addition a subordinate source of law which is drawn-up under powers specifically delegated by particular statutes. (For instance 'statutory instruments' are a main source of this 'secondary' legislation, often containing the 'small-print' of a statute). There is no written constitution in England whereby a Supreme Court is empowered to declare a blatantly unfair Act of Parliament invalid (such as exists in the USA). (Also note that in the US each state has its own law-making powers and justice system. There is however an over-riding system of 'Federal law' as well as a more centralised appeal court system consisting of an Appeals Court and ultimately the Supreme Court.)

Case-law

There is a general principle in English law that courts must interpret the wording of legislation literally (i.e. by attributing the literal meaning to each word, regardless of how perverse an interpretation that may lead to). Courts are provided with some assistance in interpreting the meaning and intended purpose of legislation. E.g.

- The statute may provide definitions of words or clauses used within the statute
- The Interpretation Act 1978 (which provides definitions for a range of standard words and phrases commonly used in statutes)
- English dictionaries
- Hansard (transcripts of the actual debates by members of Parliament concerning the particular legislation and its enactment)

English courts are required to interpret legislation in accordance with the Human Rights Act 1998. They are also required to interpret statutes in accordance with European Union law. This means that UK courts are now adopting the European approach to interpretation (i.e. by interpreting legislation in light of the intended purpose of the legislation as opposed to purely on a literal interpretation).

There are many instances however in which the intended purpose or specific meaning of legislation is in doubt and has to be further interpreted. Similarly, the law often has to be interpreted in relation to specific circumstances. It is the courts which then interpret the law. In doing so, an English court adheres to the doctrine of *binding precedent*. This is a concept whereby a Judge is bound to rule consistently with previous decisions by a higher court on similar points of law and circumstances when making a finding in a particular case. It is very unusual however for two cases to be exactly the same in terms of facts and circumstances and lawyers will often try therefore to *distinguish* a previous court decision which is adverse to their particular case. If satisfied that the present can be distinguished from an earlier case (i.e. a precedent) then the precedent need not be binding on the present case in regard to determining its decision.

Areas of law

In broad terms, English law can be classified into *civil law* and *criminal law*.

Civil law

Civil law is concerned with the legal rights and obligations of individuals and organisations in relation to each other and includes a wide range of law including:

- tort law (e.g. the car crash case in Chapter 8)
- contract (e.g. the case in Chapter 7)
- employment law (Chapter 10)
- land law
- company and commercial law.

Thus the remedy in civil law usually involves monetary compensation, i.e. damages and/or some other remedy such as an injunction.

Criminal law

Criminal law addresses law enforcement in the sense of the state or police authority *prosecuting* individuals or organizations for having committed crimes. Crimes can involve violence, for instance grievous bodily harm (GBH) and murder. A crime can also be committed in the course of commercial activity however, such as by committing fraud. In criminal law a Defendant is *charged* with a crime and *prosecuted*. The *prosecution* is brought by a *prosecutor*. The Defendant will *plead guilty* or *not guilty*. He or she will then be found *guilty or not guilty* by the court, being *convicted* if found *guilty* and *acquitted* if found *not guilty*. Rather than damages being awarded the Defendant will then be *sentenced* by way of *punishment*. (Although the court may also make a *compensation order*, requiring the convicted person to pay some monetary compensation to his *victim*.)

The court system

Civil courts

The High Court
The High Court of England and Wales consists of three divisions, namely:

Chancery (Ch) Division; Family Division; Queen's Bench (QB) Division.

The Chancery Division hears actions such as bankruptcy, copyright and mortgage cases. The Family Division deals with matrimonial cases, i.e. divorce etc. The Queen's Bench Division deals with higher value and more complex civil cases (such as tort cases for personal injury worth over £50,000) and breach of contract cases (such as the case of *Travelgraph* v *Matrix Printers* in Chapter 7).

The County Court
There are approximately 250 County Courts throughout England and Wales. They generally handle lesser value civil claims (e.g. personal injury cases worth under £50,000 and breach of contract claims up to £15,000).

Tribunals
There are a range of tribunals for various matters such as immigration, rent reviews and employment law cases. The latter are known as Employment Tribunals (you considered an Employment Tribunal case in Chapter 10).

Court of Appeal (civil division)
Hears appeals from the lower courts, i.e. County and High Courts.

House of Lords
Ultimate UK appeal court. Appeals to the House of Lords (HL) are only possible on a point of law. A HL case is usually heard by five 'Lords of Appeal in ordinary' (more commonly referred to as 'Law Lords').

European Court of Justice
A court or tribunal may refer a case to the European Court of Justice (ECJ) for clarification of any aspect of EU law if necessary in order to deliver its judgment.

Criminal courts

Magistrates' Courts
Generally hear less serious criminal cases

Crown Courts
Crown Court cases are heard in front of a Judge and jury, the Judge adjudicating and directing on the law and a jury deciding on the facts of the case. Crown Courts also hear appeals from Magistrates' Courts.

Court of Appeal (criminal division)
Hears appeals from the Crown Court

House of Lords

Final appeal venue for criminal cases. (Appeal must be on a point of law.)

Finding the law

UK statutes are published by Her Majesty's Stationery Office (HMSO) as well as in publications such as *Halsbury's Statutes* (which summarises and explains English law in straightforward English). There are also various series of law reports including *The All England Law Reports* (All ER) and *The Weekly Law Reports* (WLR). (A law report is a transcript of the court's decision in a particular case). Quality newspapers such as *The Times* and *The Financial Times* regularly report cases in abbreviated form. Developing the habit of reading law reports will assist in further developing your vocabulary. Electronic sources via the internet are however an increasingly effective way of conducting legal research. Some of the most useful of these sources are therefore provided in the following section.

Electronic sources

A number of 'on-line' resources are fee-paying subscription services. However a wide range of legal databases are available free on-line. The following is a non-exhaustive list of legal resources available free on the internet. You should however always satisfy yourself of the suitability of the sources you access.

www.curia.eu.int (ECJ judgments)

www.hmso.gov.uk

www.parliament.uk

www.lawreports.co.uk

www.courtservice.gov.uk (Court forms and judgments etc)

www.companieshouse.org.uk/

www.thelawyer.com/

There are also a number of 'link-sites' and 'gate-ways' which may assist in locating useful legal websites. For instance:

www.ials.sas.ac.uk/eagle-i.htm (Institute of Advanced Legal Studies)

www.venables.co.uk/legal

www.bailii.org

www.barcouncil.org.uk (The Bar Council)

www.lawsociety.org.uk/home.law (The Law Society)

www.law.cam.ac.uk/jurist/index.htm

Law analysis and study

When researching law or undertaking the study of law (whether at undergraduate or post-graduate level) you will obviously encounter statutes and case-law.

Reading statutes

The excerpt on p. 156 shows the first page of a typical statute, namely the Human Rights Act 1998. Most statutes are referred to by their 'short title' in this way. The longer title which follows then describes in more detail the purpose and aims of the statute.

Reading case-law

Note carefully the name of the case. This includes the names of the parties (Claimant's name followed by Defendant's name) followed by what is known as the *citation*. This normally includes the year of the case report along with details of the volume / page number of the law report series where the report can be located. When referring to a case it is necessary to cite the case, in other words provide the case citation, for example: *Series 5 Software Ltd* v *Clarke (1996) 1 All ER 853* (indicating the names of the parties and where the case can be found, i.e. in volume 1 of the *All England Law Reports* at page 853).

When reading a case also note carefully the court which decided the case (taking account of its authority, i.e. is it a High Court or a House of Lords decision). Many case reports have a *headnote* which can be very useful since this provides a summary of the facts and decision. It will also set out the fundamental legal principles on which the judgment is based (known as the *ratio decidendi*).

When writing coursework etc. grammar remains important, as does the need to use plain English which is clear in meaning and concise. As a general rule however remember that academic English involves using the 'third person' (e.g. 'he', 'they' and 'it' etc. as opposed to 'I' or 'you' etc.) and the 'passive' voice instead of the 'active' voice.

Finally, keep a written record of your legal research. The following form may assist you with this.

RESEARCH SHEET

Summary of the purpose of the research

Search words (identify here the main area of law or subject of the problem – e.g. if researching law concerning car crashes words such as 'personal injury', 'tort','negligence' and 'accident' would be relevant search words)

Research trail (details of cases read and other legal materials read such as statutes and their sources)

Details of research findings and conclusions

ELIZABETH II   c. 42

Human Rights Act 1998   ← Short title of statute

1998 CHAPTER 42

An Act to give further effect to rights and freedoms guaranteed
under the European Convention on Human Rights; to make
provision with respect to holders of certain judicial offices who   ← Long title of statute,
become judges of the European Court of Human Rights; and for   describing the purpose
connected purposes.   [9th November 1998]   and aims of the
                                                                       statute.

BE IT ENACTED by the Queen's most Excellent Majesty, by and with
the advice and consent of the Lords Spiritual and Temporal, and
Commons, in this present Parliament assembled, and by the
authority of the same, as follows:—

Introduction

1.—(1) In this Act "the Convention rights" means the rights and   The Convention
fundamental freedoms set out in—   Rights.

    (a) Articles 2 to 12 and 14 of the Convention,

    (b) Articles 1 to 3 of the First Protocol, and

    (c) Articles 1 and 2 of the Sixth Protocol,

as read with Articles 16 to 18 of the Convention.

(2) Those Articles are to have effect for the purposes of this Act subject
to any designated derogation or reservation (as to which see sections 14
and 15).

(3) The Articles are set out in Schedule 1.

(4) The Secretary of State may by order make such amendments to this
Act as he considers appropriate to reflect the effect, in relation to the
United Kingdom, of a protocol.

(5) In subsection (4) "protocol" means a protocol to the Convention—

    (a) which the United Kingdom has ratified; or

    (b) which the United Kingdom has signed with a view to ratification.

(6) No amendment may be made by an order under subsection (4) so
as to come into force before the protocol concerned is in force in relation
to the United Kingdom.

Appendix 2
Glossary

The following is a glossary (guide) of legal terminology. Please note however that this glossary is for guidance only and is not intended as an exhaustive or comprehensive source of definitions. The meanings provided are those commonly associated with the words and phrases in a legal context and it should be borne in mind that those same words and phrases may have a different meaning in a different context.

Acknowledgement of Service Court form used by a party to legal proceedings to confirm receipt of a Statement of Case (such as a claim form).

Acquittal A finding by a court of not guilty to a criminal charge.

Action Legal proceedings / Claim.

Advocacy Representing a party by means of spoken submission to a court or tribunal.

Advocate A court lawyer.

Affidavit A written statement sworn on oath.

Agenda An itinerary or list of matters for discussion at a meeting.

Aggravated Damages Additional compensation awarded by a court to compensate for particularly objectionable conduct on the part of the Defendant.

Agreement Contract or arrangement agreed orally or in writing between different parties.

Alibi A defence to a criminal charge based on the contention that the accused was elsewhere when the crime is alleged to have been committed.

Appeal Challenge to the validity or correctness of a decision of a court or tribunal (usually based on the contention that the law was incorrectly interpreted).

Appellant Term used to describe a party appealing against a court or tribunal decision.

Applicant Person or organisation commencing Employment Tribunal proceedings or making an application to court for a specific remedy prior to trial.

Arrest The physical seizure of an individual (normally by a policeman) on suspicion of a crime having been committed by that individual or to prevent a crime being committed.

Attorney American term for lawyer.

Bail The release of an individual from police custody pending further appearance by that person in court or at a police station.

Barrister A lawyer who is a specialist court advocate and referred to as 'counsel' (often being instructed by a solicitor to appear in court on behalf of a client).

Brief to Counsel Set of instructions prepared by a solicitor and provided to a barrister, setting out details of a case (including relevant facts and law etc.) to enable the barrister to provide representation in court on behalf of a client.

Burden of Proof Term used to indicate which party the onus is placed on to establish or prove a case and to what degree. E.g. in a civil case the burden of proof is on the Claimant to establish the case on the 'balance

158

of probabilities' (whereas in a criminal case the prosecution must normally establish the case beyond all reasonable doubt).

Case-law   Law created by court decisions, i.e. law created by cases which provide precedents of relevance for future legal disputes (see 'Precedent' below).

Cause of Action   The legal grounds or basis of a claim or 'action' commenced in court (e.g. breach of contract).

Case   A legal dispute between specific parties.

Certificate of Incorporation   Certificate issued by the Registrar of Companies confirming that a company has been incorporated (i.e. legally recognised as having been created).

Chambers   Has two main meanings: (1) to refer to a hearing in private as opposed to in open court (ref. to as being 'in chambers') and (2) to refer to a barrister's place of work ('counsel's chambers').

Charge   Allegation (usually in writing) of specific criminal conduct against an individual. (That individual is then said to have been 'charged' – such as with theft for instance.)

Civil Action / Proceedings   Legal action based on a civil right (as opposed to a criminal action) such as breach of contract, for instance.

Claim Form   Court form used to commence legal proceedings in court.

Class Action   A legal action commenced in the name of one or a few named Claimants on behalf of a class of Claimants.

Client   Term used by lawyers to refer to their 'customers'.

Common Law   Legal rules and principles founded on court decisions as opposed to statutes or similar written laws or regulations.

Conference with Counsel   Meeting between a barrister and a client (usually in the presence of a solicitor).

Contempt of Court   Refusal or failure to comply with a court order or requirement.

Contingency Fees   Fees charged by a lawyer for legal work which are based on a percentage of the damages recovered on behalf of that client. (Generally only permissible in the USA albeit contingency fees can be charged in Employment Tribunal cases in the UK.)

Contract   A legally enforceable agreement.

Contributory Negligence   Degree to which a Claimant is deemed to have contributed to or caused the accident or degree of injury for which damages are being claimed. (Damages can be reduced to reflect this degree of contributory negligence.)

Conviction   A finding by a court or tribunal that an individual is guilty of the offence charged. (That person is then said to have been 'convicted' of the offence charged – e.g. theft.)

Corroboration   Evidence from an independent source which substantiates a party's version of events.

Costs   Term used to refer to legal costs or expenses of legal work conducted by lawyers on behalf of clients.

Counsel   Term used to refer to a barrister. (Barristers awarded the distinction of being known as 'Queen's Counsel' are known as 'senior counsel'; also a term in the US for an attorney.)

Counsel's Opinion   Legal advice proposed by a barrister.

Counterclaim   A claim by a Defendant in legal proceedings who in turn alleges that he has a legal claim against the Claimant.

County Court   Civil court which usually deals with lower value civil cases.

Court List   List or schedule prepared by a court which provides details of the date and time that each trial or hearing is scheduled for.

Criminal Injuries Compensation Authority (CICA)   A Government scheme to provide monetary compensation to victims of crimes of violence.

Cross-Examination Questioning of a witness in court by a party other than the party calling that particular witness to provide evidence.

Crown Court Criminal court of the Supreme Court of England and Wales with jurisdiction over the most serious criminal cases. (There are a number of Crown Courts located throughout England and Wales.)

Custodial Sentence A sentence of imprisonment by a court or tribunal.

Damages Monetary compensation (such as for personal injury).

Defence Statement of case setting out the legal grounds and details on which a Defendant is defending legal proceedings being pursued against that Defendant.

Defendant The party to legal proceedings against whom the claim is being made by the Claimant.

Deposition A written or recorded witness statement taken on oath.

Directions A list of steps or instructions, usually issued by a court, setting out the specific actions which each party in a legal action is required to comply with prior to the case being heard in court. (In order to ensure that the legal proceedings concerned proceed efficiently and that the parties in the case have properly prepared their cases in readiness for trial.)

Director Individual with management responsibilities within a company. (All directors of a company are collectively referred to as the 'board of directors'.)

Disbursements Costs incurred in the course of legal work other than a solicitor's fees (e.g. travelling expenses and fees payable to expert witnesses).

Discontinuance A situation whereby the Claimant in civil proceedings voluntarily confirms that the case is no longer being pursued (i.e. is being 'discontinued').

Disclosure Revealing to another party to legal proceedings the past or present existence of evidential material (usually documents) which may be relevant to the case.

Discovery The process whereby each party to legal proceedings reveals details of documentation and information in their possession which may be relevant to the case. (Thereby providing another party in the case with the opportunity to inspect or obtain copies of such material. The court usually orders that discovery should take place simultaneously between the parties.)

District Judge A judicial officer of the County Court who acts as judge in many straightforward County Court cases.

Documentary Evidence Evidence in written form (e.g. letters and contracts etc.).

Evidence Information and material (such as witness testimony and documentation) relevant to a case and on which a court or tribunal bases its findings.

Evidence in Chief Evidence elicited from a witness by the party calling that witness.

Examination in Chief Questioning of a witness in court by the party calling that particular witness to give evidence.

Exemplary Damages Additional compensation awarded by a court amounting to more than the actual losses sustained by a party and intended as a penalty to reflect the court's particular disapproval of the Defendant's conduct. (Usually only awarded in US courts, where some exemplary damages awards have amounted to hundreds of millions of dollars.)

Ex parte A hearing in court which takes place with one of the parties to the proceedings being absent. (A more modern equivalent phrase now commonly used is 'without notice'.)

Expert Witness Witness called to provide evidence involving professional expertise in a particular field which is relevant to a particular case (e.g. a doctor).

Express Term Term or provision in an agreement which is specifically (i.e. expressly) stated or written.

Extraordinary General Meeting Any general (shareholders') meeting of a company other than its Annual General Meeting (AGM).

Further and Better Particulars More specific detail or information of a specific aspect of the case referred to in the statements of case (court documents). (Such further detail or information will usually be provided in response to a request by a party for such further detail or information in order to clarify the claim being made.)

General Damages Compensation which can only be determined by reference to previous cases of a similar nature or by the court (including for instance damages for pain and suffering).

High Court Civil court which deals with higher value civil cases.

I.e. Abbreviation for Latin phrase 'id est' and meaning 'that is' or 'in other words'.

Illegal Against the law. (E.g. stealing is illegal.)

Implied Term Term of an agreement not expressly stated but recognised in law by virtue of the obvious understanding between the parties or by their conduct or the circumstances of the agreement. (An implied term can also be imposed by statute, e.g. implied term of satisfactory quality.)

In Camera In private. (E.g. a court hearing closed to the public is sometimes referred to as being 'in camera'.)

Injunction A court order compelling a person to do or refrain from doing something.

In Open Court A trial or court hearing in public.

Instructions to Counsel Written information prepared by a solicitor and provided to a barrister to enable that barrister to provide advice to a client or to draft legal documentation on behalf of a client. Such 'instructions to counsel' usually include a summary of the facts of the case, relevant law and any relevant supporting documentation.

Interim Order An order made by a court prior to the final trial or hearing of a particular case (e.g. an order for directions setting out the further steps each party is required to take prior to trial).

Interlocutory Application / Hearing / Order An application to court, court hearing or court order made prior to trial.

Inter partes Term used to refer to a court hearing at which all parties are present (as opposed to an 'ex-parte' hearing at which at least one party is absent).

Interrogatory A request for further information.

Issue (of Proceedings) To commence legal proceedings by lodging relevant papers at court (such as a claim form). (This is referred to as 'issuing proceedings'.)

Judge Trier or adjudicator of a case responsible for making findings of law (and sometimes of fact albeit also see 'jury' below).

Judg(e)ment A decision or declaration of the court, usually setting out the court's findings and details of any damages (compensation) or other remedy which the court has decided to grant to any party in the case.

Jurisdiction The authority to decide and enforce the law. (E.g. the County and High Courts have jurisdiction to try breach of contract cases in England and Wales.)

Jury Group of individuals (usually 12) who make findings of fact in the most serious criminal cases (usually in the Crown Court in England and Wales).

Intellectual Property Law relating to copyright, rights to inventions (patents) and trademarks etc.

Law A system of rules and regulations governing and determining permissible conduct within society.

Leading Question A question which suggests the answer or which implies the existence of some particular fact(s) or circumstances.

Leave Permission. (E.g. to seek 'leave of the court' is to seek permission of the court.)

Legal Privilege A legal right to refuse to disclose or produce documentation or other evidence on the basis of some special interest recognised by law. (Typically relating to the legally recognised right for discussions and correspondence between lawyer and client to remain 'privileged' and thus protected from disclosure.)

Letter Before Action Correspondence sent by a prospective Claimant or his legal advisor intimating to another party an intention to commence legal action against that other party along with brief details of the proposed legal action. (Note that a more modern equivalent is 'letter of claim'.)

Letter of Claim Modern term for 'letter before action' (see above).

Liability Legal responsibility to comply with or discharge a legal obligation or indebtedness.

Limitation Period The time-limit prescribed by law in which a Claimant must commence a claim in court. Failure to issue the claim in court within this time-limit will usually result in the Claimant losing the legal right to pursue that particular claim. (E.g. the limitation period for a personal injury claim is three years in the UK.)

Listing for Trial Procedure for providing the court with final documentation and information in order to enable the court to finalise a date for trial.

Litigant A party to legal proceedings (i.e. to litigation – see below).

Litigation Legal action / proceedings involving a dispute between parties.

Liquidated Damages A term used to refer to a specifically quantifiable amount of monetary compensation which a Claimant is seeking from another party. (I.e. a sum which can be precisely calculated as opposed to an amount which is variable at the court's discretion.)

Locus Location of an incident, particularly of an accident.

Magistrates' Court Criminal Court in England and Wales which tries the relatively less serious criminal cases. (Usually conducted by a 'Magistrate'.)

Member A company shareholder.

Minutes Record of matters discussed and decided in the course of directors' and shareholders' meetings.

Minor An individual under 18 years of age.

Mitigation A term used in criminal law to refer to submissions seeking to justify or at least provide some explanation for a party's conduct and aimed at persuading a court or tribunal to show some sympathy towards that party. (See also 'Mitigation of Damages' below.)

Mitigation of Damages A term used in civil law to refer to efforts made by a Claimant to minimise or alleviate loss and damage sustained.

Negligence Used in a legal sense to refer to a failure to comply with a duty of care towards others imposed by law or by generally accepted standards.

Oral Evidence Spoken (as opposed to documentary) evidence.

Party Person or organisation entering into an agreement or engaged in legal proceedings.

Plaintiff Person or party commencing a legal action. Note that the term 'Claimant' is now used in English courts in place of 'Plaintiff' (the term 'Plaintiff' still being in general use however in American courts).

Pleadings A term previously used to refer to the court documents setting out each party's case and now largely superseded by the term 'Statements of Case'.

Poll Means of voting at shareholders' meetings whereby votes on a particular resolution are counted on the basis of the number of voting shares held by each person voting (as opposed to 'on a show of hands').

Precedent Existing document, draft or court decision which is relevant to and used as the basis for subsequent legal drafting or decisions. ('Doctrine of Precedent' refers to a concept whereby previous court decisions establish the general legal position for subsequent legal disputes involving similar circumstances.)

Privilege (See 'Legal Privilege' above.)

Proceedings Term used to refer to an ongoing court action (known as court or legal proceedings).

Proxy An individual appointed to represent a shareholder at a shareholders' meeting.

Quantum (of Damages) The level or amount of monetary compensation (damages) awarded by a court or agreed between the parties to a case by negotiation.

Quash Over-rule or annul a previous court decision.

Queen's Counsel A title bestowed on barristers who have demonstrated a high level of professional expertise and competence. Barristers appointed as 'Queen's Counsel' may use the letters 'QC' after their names and are sometimes referred to as 'silks' or 'Leading Counsel'.

Quorum Minimum number required to be present at a meeting in order for decisions taken at that meeting to be valid.

Registered Office Official address of a company as recorded with the Registrar of Companies at which official documents and legal proceedings can be served on a company.

Registrar of Companies Official responsible for maintaining the 'Company Registry' recording details of incorporated companies.

Remedy The specific means by which a party receives restitution or satisfaction for loss caused by another. (E.g. the usual remedy for personal injury is damages.)

Resolution A decision made by members of a company.

Respondent Person defending an application to court for a specific order or defending Employment Tribunal proceedings.

Return Date Date set by a court for an interlocutory hearing.

Restrictive Covenant Clause to prevent an employee competing etc. with his / her employer.

Rights of Audience Right to appear in and address a particular court or tribunal.

Service Provision or delivery of court documentation (such as a claim form or notice of a forthcoming court hearing etc.). A person receiving such documentation is referred to as having been 'served'.

Set Aside A subsequent order or direction from a court cancelling a previous judgment or order (referred to as 'setting aside' the previous order or direction).

Setting Down for Trial Now usually referred to as 'listing for trial'. (See 'Listing for Trial' above.)

Settlement An agreement reached between parties to a legal dispute which concludes that dispute.

Shareholder Owner of shares in a company (i.e. who is a 'member' of that company).

Solicitor A lawyer who prepares cases and legal transactions on behalf of a client (often instructing a barrister to provide representation in court).

Special Damages Actual financial losses which can be specifically ascertained as having been incurred between the date the cause of action arose and the date of trial. (E.g. loss of earnings up to trial and property damage sustained etc.)

Standard of Proof The criterion or degree of proof required in order for a party to establish its case. (E.g. in civil cases the standard of proof is 'on the balance of probabilities' whereas in a criminal case it is usually 'beyond all reasonable doubt'.)

Statute Legislation in the form of written laws and regulations (such as 'Acts of Parliament' created by the UK Parliament).

Stay A halt to court proceedings. Proceedings which are thus 'stayed' do not continue any further (although a stay can subsequently be 'lifted' to enable those proceedings to continue).

Strike Out To 'strike out' means that the court has ordered that a particular aspect of a case (such as particular written details in a statement of case) is to be removed from the court records and can therefore no longer be relied upon. The court can strike out an entire case if a party is sufficiently dilatory in complying with steps required by the court, thereby effectively terminating those proceedings.

Subpoena Witness summons requiring a witness to attend court to give evidence.

Sue Informal term meaning to issue legal proceedings.

Testimony Statement or assertion made to a court by a witness.

Tort A breach of a duty imposed by civil law (e.g. negligence).

Unliquidated Damages Damages (monetary compensation) which cannot be precisely quantified upon commencement of legal proceedings (as opposed to liquidated damages which can–see above).

Vicarious Liability A legal concept whereby a person or entity can be held liable for the fault or wrongdoing of another. (A typical example of this is an employer being liable for the negligence of an employee acting in the course of his employment, i.e. vicariously liable.)

Without Prejudice A legal concept whereby oral or written communication can be entered into between parties with a view to reaching a negotiated settlement. I.e. on the basis that the details of such communication cannot be disclosed to the court or relied upon in court in the event that a settlement is not achieved.

Writ Court form traditionally used to commence legal proceedings in court. (Note that claim forms are now used far more commonly for commencing legal proceedings.)

Appendix 3
Answer key

Chapter 1

Exercise 2

1. Each shareholder's liability is limited to the amount, if any, unpaid on the shares held by him / her
2. £50,000
3. Form 10; Form 12; Memorandum of Association; Articles of Association
4. The Memorandum and Articles of Association
5. No – a sole director cannot also be the company secretary
6. Certificate of Incorporation

Exercise 3

Memorandum of Association

(1) Maplink Limited
(2) Maplink Limited
(3) limited
(4) £250,000
(5) DIMITRIS YAVAPRAPAS, THE MANOR, 2 QUEEN ELIZABETH STREET, LONDON, SE1 5NP
(6) GISELA WIRTH, 15 ROBIN HOOD WAY, MANSFIELD, NOTTINGHAM, NG2 7CX
(7) TWENTY-FIVE THOUSAND
(8) TWO HUNDRED AND FIFTY THOUSAND

Form 10

Companies House
— for the record —

10

Please complete in typescript,
or in bold black capitals.
CHWP000

Notes on completion appear on final page

First directors and secretary and intended situation of registered office

Company Name in full | MAPLINK LIMITED

Proposed Registered Office | 44 PRINCESS DIANA WALK
(PO Box numbers only, are not acceptable)

Post town | SOUTH KENSINGTON

County / Region | LONDON | Postcode | W2 3SL

If the memorandum is delivered by an agent for the subscriber(s) of the memorandum mark the box opposite and give the agent's name and address.

Agent's Name

Address

Post town

County / Region | Postcode

Number of continuation sheets attached

You do not have to give any contact information in the box opposite but if you do, it will help Companies House to contact you if there is a query on the form. The contact information that you give will be visible to searchers of the public record.

Tel

DX number | DX exchange

Companies House receipt date barcode
This form has been provided free of charge by Companies House

v 08/02

When you have completed and signed the form please send it to the Registrar of Companies at:
Companies House, Crown Way, Cardiff, CF14 3UZ   DX 33050 Cardiff
for companies registered in England and Wales
or
Companies House, 37 Castle Terrace, Edinburgh, EH1 2EB
for companies registered in Scotland   DX 235 Edinburgh
or LP - 4 Edinburgh 2

Company Secretary (see notes 1-5)

	Company name	MAPLINK LIMITED
NAME	*Style / Title	MISS
	*Honours etc	

* Voluntary details

Forename(s)	GISELA
Surname	WIRTH
Previous forename(s)	
Previous surname(s)	

†† Tick this box if the address shown is a service address for the beneficiary of a Confidentiality Order granted under section 723B of the Companies Act 1985 otherwise, give your usual residential address. In the case of a corporation or Scottish firm, give the registered or principal office address.

Address ††	15 ROBIN HOOD WAY
	MANSFIELD
Post town	NOTTINGHAM
County / Region	
Postcode	NG2 7CX
Country	U.K.

I consent to act as secretary of the company named on page 1

Consent signature		Date	

Directors (see notes 1-5)

Please list directors in alphabetical order

NAME	*Style / Title	MR.
	*Honours etc	

Forename(s)	THOMAS
Surname	SHAPIRO
Previous forename(s)	
Previous surname(s)	

†† Tick this box if the address shown is a service address for the beneficiary of a Confidentiality Order granted under section 723B of the Companies Act 1985 otherwise, give your usual residential address. In the case of a corporation or Scottish firm, give the registered or principal office address.

Address ††	23 ESSEX STREET
Post town	HAMPTON COURT
County / Region	
Postcode	KT8 1NQ
Country	U.K.

	Day	Month	Year	
Date of birth	2 0 2	1 9 6 8		Nationality

Business occupation	BARRISTER
Other directorships	

I consent to act as director of the company named on page 1

Consent signature		Date	

167

Directors (see notes 1-5)

Please list directors in alphabetical order

NAME	*Style / Title	PROFESSOR

*Honours etc

* Voluntary details

Forename(s)	DIMITRIS
Surname	YAVAPRAPAS
Previous forename(s)	
Previous surname(s)	

†† Tick this box if the address shown is a service address for the beneficiary of a Confidentiality Order granted under section 723B of the Companies Act 1985 otherwise, give your usual residential address. In the case of a corporation or Scottish firm, give the registered or principal office address.

Address ††

	THE MANOR
	2 QUEEN ELIZABETH STREET
Post town	LONDON
County / Region		Postcode	SE1 5NP
Country	U.K.

Date of birth

Day	Month	Year
0 3	0 7	1 9 5 4

Nationality

Business occupation SURGEON

Other directorships

I consent to act as director of the company named on page 1

Consent signature | | **Date** |

This section must be signed by either an agent on behalf of all subscribers or the subscribers (i.e those who signed as members on the memorandum of association).	Signed		Date	
	Signed		Date	
	Signed		Date	
	Signed		Date	
	Signed		Date	
	Signed		Date	
	Signed		Date	

Form 12

(1) Maplink Limited

(2) Stringwood & Evans, 18 Bond Street, London, W1 1KR; Tel – 020 7538 2892 – DX Number 12432 – DX Exchange London 1

Exercise 4

1. appeal against
2. went against
3. decide against
4. enter into
5. negotiate with
6. act for

Chapter 2

Exercise 1

1. (c) resolved	**4.** (c) presented	**7.** (d) resolutions
2. (b) appointed	**5.** (b) convened	**8.** (a) declared
3. (d) registered	**6.** (b) provided	

Exercise 2

1. Conducting (or holding) a meeting
2. Over 50% of the votes cast
3. This means that each person present at the meeting has one vote, votes being counted on a 'show of hands'
4. To avoid the need for directors to travel to attend a meeting in a particular place (which may be particularly inconvenient for instance if some directors are based abroad)
5. For any reason connected with the management of the company. E.g. to consider appointing further directors or to change the name of the company
6. The minimum number required to be present in order for decisions taken at the meeting to be valid

Chapter 3

Exercise 2

(1) Notice	**(3)** passing	**(5)** special
(2) for the purpose of	**(4)** resolutions	**(6)** appointed

Continued

| (7) Travelgraph | (9) vote |
| (8) convene | (10) member |

Exercise 3

(1) noted	(5) director	(9) show
(2) declared	(6) chairman	(10) closed
(3) proposed	(7) unanimously	
(4) ordinary	(8) special	

Exercise 4

1. The vote being 100% for or against the resolution
2. Member of a company
3. A situation whereby the number of votes for and against a resolution are exactly the same
4. An additional vote, usually provided to the chairman in the event that there is a deadlock of votes (as referred to in question 3 above). The casting vote is then used to break such a deadlock (but cannot be used to create a deadlock)
5. To arrange / provide notice of a meeting
6. No. (However it is permissible for a company to stipulate in its articles that, in order to qualify to become a director, an individual must own a specified minimum shareholding)
7. 14 days
8. 21 days – because a special resolution (to change the name of the company) is being proposed at the meeting and a special resolution requires 21 days' notice. (Note however that this notice requirement can be avoided provided at least 95% of the shareholders agree to shorter notice)
9. Any member entitled to vote at the meeting may appoint someone else (who need not be a shareholder) to go along to the meeting and vote on their behalf. The notice calling an extraordinary general meeting (EGM) must make clear that each member has the right to appoint a proxy. (Note that there is a growing trend for notices of company meetings to be provided to members electronically)

Exercise 5

(1) in	(4) regarding	(7) to
(2) of	(5) by	(8) From
(3) with	(6) from	

Exercise 6

Form 288a

(1) 04041969
(2) Kadir
(3) Salleh
(4) 4 Kensington Palace Gardens
(5) London
(6) W2 4AJ
(7) United Kingdom

Form NC 19

(1) Maplink Limited
(2) Extraordinary General (delete Annual General / General)
(3) 44 Princess Diana Walk, South Kensington, London, W2 3SL
(4) 15th day of May 2006
(5) Travelgraph Limited

■ Chapter 4

Exercise 1

1. 10 July 2006 (clause 2.1)
2. three years (clause 2.1)
3. to promote and develop business (clause 3.1.1)
4. £75,000 per annum (clause 4.1)
5. company vehicle (clause 5) and pension scheme (clause 6)
6. yes – there is a restraint of trade clause preventing Kadir Salleh from competing for 12 months (clause 9)
7. English law (clause 10)
8. He does not hold any shares in the company despite being a director. A *Bushell* v *Faith* clause would not therefore be of any assistance to him

Exercise 2

1. service agreement
2. terms and conditions
3. definitions
4. employment
5. remuneration
6. entitlement
7. confidentiality
8. intellectual property
9. restraint of trade
10. jurisdiction

Exercise 3

(1) Section 303	(10) ordinary	(19) remove
(2) shareholders	(11) vote	(20) ordinary
(3) director	(12) representations	(21) compensation
(4) resolution	(13) shareholders	(22) breach of contract
(5) majority	(14) voted	(23) notice
(6) shares	(15) notice	(24) removal
(7) resolution	(16) meeting	(25) negotiating
(8) shareholding	(17) agreement	(26) settlement / agreement
(9) pass	(18) fixed-term	

Exercise 4

1. shareholders	3. representations	5. ordinary resolution
2. shareholding	4. shareholders' meeting	6. fixed-term contract

Exercise 5

1. another agreement
2. can protect a company's trade secrets
3. English law
4. a breach of contract claim
5. per s. 303 Companies Act 1985

Chapter 5

Exercise 1

Task 1

1. false	2. true	3. true	4. false

Task 2

1. Many 'high street' brands – e.g. McDonald's and Kentucky Fried Chicken (KFC)
2. commission
3. From the 'mark-up' between the price paid to the supplier and the sales price to the distributor's ultimate customer
4. Sharing of risk / cost / knowledge / skills etc.

Exercise 2

(1) hereby	(4) furthermore	(7) In addition
(2) further	(5) hereby	(8) during
(3) Moreover	(6) henceforth	(9) within

Exercise 3

Task 1

This agreement shall continue in force / for a period of two years save and except that it may / be terminated by either party providing to the other / three calendar months notice in writing.

Task 2

In the event that / the Agent fails to achieve a minimum total sales amount of / £750,000 within / twelve months of the commencement of this Agreement / the Principal shall be entitled / to terminate this Agreement / by notifying the Agent in writing accordingly.

Exercise 4

(a) Suggested draft:

The Principal further agrees to pay a bonus to the Agent amounting to 1% of total net sales in the event that: the agent achieves sales exceeding £1,250,000 within the first year from commencement of this Agreement.

(b)

At the end of clause 4 entitled 'REMUNERATION', possibly adding a further paragraph marked '4.2'.

▊ Chapter 6

Exercise 2

(1) Travelgraph Limited	(4) Solicitor	(7) sent to prison
(2) Kadir Salleh	(5) set aside this order	(8) Respondent
(3) prohibits you from doing (delete 'obliges you to do')	(6) Contempt of Court	(9) Worldlink Limited

Continued

(10) Worldlink Limited	(13) to the Court	(16) Name – Stringwood & Evans ; Address – 18 Bond Street, London, W1 1KR ; Tel No – 020 7538 2892
(11) confidential information relating to Travelgraph	(14) Order	
(12) Respondent shall pay the Applicant	(15) Applicant's	

Exercise 3

1. A situation whereby the law is unclear or has not been drafted with sufficient precision. Such a 'legal loophole' can result in the law being interpreted in a way which results in possible evasion of the purpose or protection which the law was intended to provide.
2. This means that the court order or legal document has been drafted to cover every possible eventuality and to prevent the purpose of the order or document being defeated (such as by a 'legal loophole' as described above).
3. Jargon means professional or technical terminology used by professionals in that particular field. Legal jargon therefore refers to professional expressions commonly used by lawyers.
4. A member of the public who is not a member of a particular profession.
5. This means failing to comply with some important requirement or condition which has been imposed by a court. In practice this usually relates to being in breach of the terms of a court order.
6. A legally enforceable term (usually contained in a person's contract of employment or service contract) which prevents a person working for a competitor or competing with a former employer for a specified period of time.
7. This means that assets belonging to the Respondent can be physically taken from the Respondent by order of the Court in the event that the Respondent does not comply with the injunction order. (Including for instance in this case any computer disks or files etc. belonging to Travelgraph Limited.)

Exercise 4

1. may	2. must	3. may	4. must / should

Exercise 5

1. left	2. joined	3. has worked	4. received / consulted

Chapter 7

Exercise 1

1. Examples of types of contract include: employment; sale of goods; hire of goods; supply of services; agency; lease
2. Civil law
3. The specific details of what has been agreed between the parties (typically including price, delivery time, quantity of goods purchased and payment details etc.)
4. Implied and express
5. Law established through court decisions (see Appendix 1 for more details)
6. An Act of Parliament (see Appendix 1 for more details)
7. The Claimant
8. There is an implied term in law that goods sold in the course of a business must be of satisfactory quality. I.e. that the goods are of a standard which a reasonable person would regard as satisfactory. (Taking account for instance of matters such as how the goods were described, their price and fitness for all purposes for which goods of that type are commonly used)

Exercise 2

1. act on behalf of	4. express term	7. satisfactory proposals
2. contract	5. breach of contract	8. legal proceedings
3. our instructions	6. proposals to compensate	

Exercise 3

Old-Fashioned Language	Equivalent Modern Language
aforesaid	stated previously
aver / plead	contend / allege
in camera	in private
in open court	in public
save that / save insofar	except that
Plaintiff	claimant
pleading	statement of case
prescribed by	provided by / indicated by
undernoted	noted below
writ	claim form

Exercise 4

(1) damages	(3) Claimant	(5) recover
(2) contract	(4) claims	(6) Matrix Printers Limited

Exercise 5

The correct words or phrases (i.e. those which should *not* have been deleted) are as follows

(1) Claimant	(7) 100	(13) 50
(2) Defendant	(8) implied term	(14) loss and damage
(3) written contract	(9) Contract	(15) £200,000
(4) 1 August 2007	(10) Claimant	(16) pursuant to
(5) £45,000	(11) In breach of	(17) Claimant
(6) express term	(12) aforesaid	(18) Damages

Exercise 6

1. which / that	2. that / which	3. whom	4. who

Chapter 8

Exercise 1

1. False – (sentence 1 confirms that the writer *will* act for Nicholas Tiessen)
2. False – (the writer is a solicitor within the *Litigation Department* – paragraph 1)
3. True – (explained in paragraph 3)
4. False – (see 1st sentence in paragraph 4)
5. True – (see 2nd sentence in paragraph 4)
6. False – (see 5th paragraph)

Exercise 2

Task 1

Compound	Simple Form
in the event that	if
at a later date	later
as a consequence of	because

until such time as	until
similar to	like
at that particular time	then
prior to	before
in close proximity to	near

Task 2

Suggested answer:

American courts award higher damages in personal injury cases then English courts.

(Please note that the sentence can be re-written in alternative ways which may be equally suitable)

Exercise 3

1. Negligent driving caused the accident.
2. A consultant orthopaedic surgeon diagnosed a whiplash injury.
3. A physiotherapist is treating the Claimant.
4. A local garage will assess the extent of damage to the car.

Exercise 4

1. am having   2. was driving   3. works   4. landed

Exercise 5

Task A

1. Matthew Gluck (1st Defendant) and Londinium Delivery Company Limited (2nd Defendant)
2. Honda
3. 21 September 2007
4. At the junction between Oxford Street and Regent Street
5. Chelsea & Westminster Hospital
6. Computer programmer
7. £4,000
8. £12,000
9. Since the 1st Defendant (Matthew Gluck) was acting in the course of his employment with Londinium Delivery Company Limited when the accident occurred
10. Possible answers include: professional negligence; clinical negligence; an accident in the workplace; a train accident; an aircraft accident etc.

Exercise 6

car	accident	admissible	evidence	client's	file
legal	privilege	undisputed	facts	independent	witness

Exercise 7

take a <u>statement</u>   settle <u>out of court</u>   serve particulars <u>of claim</u>

settle the <u>case</u>   negotiate <u>settlement</u>   award <u>damages</u>

admit <u>liability</u>

Exercise 8

(1) car accident   **(3)** independent witness   **(5)** settlement proposals

(2) take a statement   **(4)** award damages   **(6)** negotiate settlement

Chapter 9

Exercise 2

Task 2

Examples include:

GOOD FACTS	BAD FACTS
Defendant does not have good eyesight	Defendant alleges traffic lights were green in his favour
Defendant has been convicted of careless driving (this will assist in establishing liability against him in the civil case)	Defendant alleges Claimant was driving too fast
Defendant drove into the side of the Claimant's vehicle, which appears to support the Claimant's version of events	Defendant alleges Claimant went through a red traffic light

Task 3

(1) am	(3) was driving	(5) was coming
(2) witnessed	(4) was	(6) heading

(7) was driving	(12) proceeded	(17) was holding
(8) was travelling	(13) began	(18) appeared
(9) approached	(14) caught	(19) came
(10) could	(15) was heading	(20) braked
(11) were showing	(16) could	

Chapter 10

Exercise 1

1. Section 94 of the Employment Rights Act 1996 provides / the legal right not to be unfairly dismissed.
2. An employee normally requires one year's service / to be eligible to claim unfair dismissal.
3. An unfair dismissal claim must be issued / within three months.
4. An unfair dismissal claim is heard at / an Employment Tribunal.
5. An employer should permit an employee to / state his case when considering dismissal.
6. An employer suspecting misconduct should / investigate the circumstances.

Exercise 2

1. 16 March 2003 and 26 April 2007
2. Legal cashier
3. Theft of client monies
4. Yes – conduct
5. The fact that he'd turned up for work driving a new Ferrari
6. Having recently won the National Lottery
7. A letter from the organisers of the National Lottery confirming his win
8. Bannerman and Law:
   failed to conduct a proper investigation prior to dismissing Charles
   did not give Charles an opportunity to provide an explanation
   did not hold a disciplinary hearing
   dismissed Charles in public
Overall there was no valid or acceptable reason for the dismissal, which was also procedurally unfair

Exercise 3

| (1) began | (3) working | (5) told |
| (2) was employed | (4) having | (6) given |

Continued

(7) arrived	(11) told	(15) dismissed
(8) driving	(12) arrived	(16) contend
(9) entering	(13) informed	(17) denied
(10) shouting	(14) explained	(18) to provide

Exercise 4

Suggested draft for Section 7 of the Notice of Appearance (Form IT3):

1. The Respondent is a city firm of solicitors with its head-office in London and four overseas offices. The firm has 40 partners and approximately 22 associate solicitors. The Respondent specialises in international corporate and commercial work.
2. On 26 April 2007 the Respondent's Managing Partner, Henry Moore, became aware that £2 million had been misappropriated from the firm's client account. It was essential that the source of this theft be ascertained without delay in order to safeguard the firm's reputation.
3. The Respondent denies that the Applicant was unfairly dismissed as alleged. The aforesaid Henry Moore made a valid managerial decision to dismiss the Applicant based on reasonable suspicion of gross misconduct. It was reasonable for Henry Moore to come to the conclusion that the Applicant had stolen the missing £2 million. The Applicant was ostentatiously displaying wealth, having arrived at work on 26 April 2007 in a new Ferrari motor car. He did not explain to the Respondent that he had won the National Lottery. The Applicant was therefore responsible for his dismissal as a result of his own actions.
4. Convening a disciplinary hearing would have been fruitless in the particular circumstances. The Applicant was therefore summarily dismissed on 26 April 2007. The Respondent had reasonable grounds to believe that the Applicant was guilty of gross misconduct. The Respondent was accordingly entitled to dismiss the Applicant, the dismissal being fair and reasonable in all the circumstances.

Exercise 5

| 1. call for the witness | 3. take down a statement |
| 2. draw up a court order | 4. sue for damages |

Exercise 6

1. strongly suggest	5. extremely fruitful	9. deliberately mislead
2. extremely generous	6. substantially increase	10. refrain from
3. solemnly declare	7. severely injured	11. dismissed without notice
4. successfully defended	8. totally objective	12. settle out of court

Exercise 7

(1) applicant	(5) dismissal	(9) mitigate
(2) Employment Tribunal	(6) disciplinary hearing	(10) award
(3) instructions	(7) misconduct	(11) damages
(4) unfairly dismissed	(8) prospects of success	(12) settlement

Exercise 8

(c) aggressive form ('A')

(d) diplomatic form ('D')

(e) aggressive form ('A')

(f) diplomatic form ('D')

Exercise 11

(Large and small markings above each group of words represent the main and lesser stress patterns, respectively.)

de-ci-sion	mis-con-duct	de-clare
pro-ced-ure	ad-mis-sion	con-si-dered
re-pre-sen-ta-tive	tri-bu-nal	hear-ing
al-le-ga-tion	con-duct	e-vi-dence
mis-a-pro-pri-a-tion	in-for-ma-tion	wrong-do-ing
dis-mis-sal	in-ves-ti-ga-tion	Re-spon-dent
fair-ness	em-ploy-er	

Exercise 12

Suggested answers:
Task 1

1. Henry Moore said that he had got the Ferrari driving swindler.
2. Scoville was told that he was being dismissed immediately.
3. He read the article in the local newspaper about the firm winning a case.
4. Charles Scoville said that he had been dismissed from his job recently.
5. The solicitor said that she would try to negotiate a settlement for him.

Task 2
1. 'How do you account for the Ferrari in the car-park?'
2. 'You are being dismissed so return the office keys immediately.'

3. 'You have a meritorious claim for unfair dismissal Mr Scoville.'

4. 'Bannerman and Law have treated Mr Scoville reprehensibly and I have no hesitation in declaring that Mr Scoville has been unfairly dismissed.'

5. 'I am pleased with the Tribunal's award of £18,000.'

Law bulletin

Text 1 – 'Which route – solicitor or barrister?'

Exercise 1

1. A barrister usually provides representation in court (i.e. is a court advocate). A solicitor is usually the first point of contact for a client and prepares the client's case, briefing a barrister to actually appear in court on behalf of the client

2. One year

3. Two years

4. Solicitors, since they usually take initial instructions from the client and brief a barrister for specific tasks, particularly to provide advocacy in court on behalf of a client

5. There are various specialist areas including: corporate work; personal injury; mergers and acquisitions; residential and commercial property; employment law; criminal law; company and commercial law

6. Factors such as the areas of work which the barrister's chambers specializes in and the type of work the barrister is instructed to undertake in the first few years of practice

7. Chambers

8. Over to you on this one!

Exercise 2

1. litigation/advocacy
2. barristers
3. billing targets
4. bar vocational
5. legal practice
6. briefed/instructed

Text 2 – 'Having cross words in the courtroom'

Exercise 3

witness	statement	cross	examination	High	Court
open	question	jury	trial	examination in	chief

Exercise 4

1. closing submissions
2. propositions
3. witnesses' evidence
4. supports your case
5. advocacy
6. cross-examiners

Text 3 – 'Asian tigers prepare to spring'

Exercise 5

1. finance and corporate
2. Japan
3. China
4. Places such as Myanmar / Laos / Cambodia
5. Foreign direct investment
6. form full partnerships with local lawyers or employ local lawyers

Exercise 6

1. fly-in, fly-out basis	3. strategy review	5. downsized
2. booming	4. withdraw	6. on the cards

Exercise 7

1. has developed	3. opened	5. showing
2. met	4. closed	6. providing

Exercise 8

Task 1

weather the storm	/	survive a difficult situation
on the cards	/	likely to happen
hit rock bottom	/	to be at the lowest point
downsized	/	reduced
hard market to crack	/	difficult market to enter
ear to the ground	/	monitor events
flavour of the month	/	currently popular

Task 2

1. on the grapevine	3. Scot free	5. bury the hatchet
2. raining cats and dogs	4. eager beaver	6. red tape

Exercise 9

Task 1

1. highest	2. least	3. most	4. fastest

Task 2

1. bigger	2. more	3. more	4. stronger

Text 4 – 'Shopping around'

Exercise 10

1. shopping around	3. to take	5. start
2. dealing	4. bringing	6. suing

Exercise 11

1. Furthermore	3. therefore	5. On the other hand
2. To begin with / firstly	4. as a result	6. however

Index

Index

Index